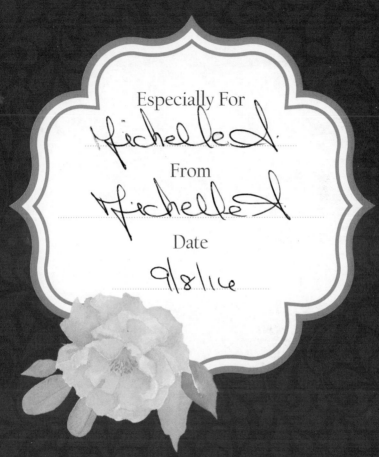

Especially For

Michelle J.

From

Michelle J.

Date

_9/8/16_

Patricia Mitchell

GOD'S BEST
for You

Devotional Inspiration
for Women

BARBOUR BOOKS
An Imprint of Barbour Publishing, Inc.

Member of the
Evangelical Christian
Publishers Association

Introduction

How can the heart draw closer to God? Where can we find inner peace, divine guidance, and genuine joy in the rush of modern-day life? What can satisfy our longing for spiritual sustenance? For assurance and stability? For values and truths that are real, relevant, and trustworthy?

These spiritual reflections invite you to grow closer to your loving God, strengthen your faith and trust in Him, and receive the joy He desires for you. . .to experience His best for you. A brief scripture verse is suggested for your personal contemplation.

As you meditate on these words and explore their applicability to your experience, you will realize that God's best for you is the same now as it always has been. Whether you're young or not so young, sitting in a cottage or skyscraper, turning a page or swiping a screen, God's message of love and grace remains unchanged. The secret of a blessed life is a relationship with Him. This brings a prayer that your relationship with Him will be deepened, strengthened, and enriched as you make these truths your own.

Jesus Christ is the same yesterday and today and forever.

HEBREWS 13:8 NIV

God's Power

Say you're put in charge of an important project. "Now," you're told, "success or failure depends on you and you alone! You'll receive no help from anyone, so you must rely solely on your own effort and know-how." While you may have looked forward to taking on the work before, you're less confident now, and with good reason.

So often, though, that's the way we approach spiritual growth. We want to find our God-given purpose, get more joy out of life, and draw closer to God, but we think it's up to us to make it happen. We might spend hours sitting still, struggling to silence our thoughts, and waiting for inspiration. When nothing happens, we lose hope of ever developing a relationship with God or of bringing peace and joy into our lives. We may even conclude that we're just not a spiritual person!

Fortunately, God has put not us, but Himself, in charge of our spiritual growth. Our creator knows we're not capable of learning who He is, how He feels about us, and what

8

He has done for us without His help. Perhaps it's our natural inability to find Him on our own that He uses to point us to Him.

If there's a desire in your heart to know God better and receive the joy He offers, let Him help you. There's no reason to struggle because He supplies you with resources, mainly the Bible, where He reveals Himself to you. He exposes you to the reflections of spiritual thinkers and the example of godly people. Most of all, He sends His Holy Spirit to you. In fact, His Spirit is at work already—your desire proves it! Now open yourself to His presence; trust Him to guide you. Go forward in confidence: God is in charge.

I want you to know about the great and mighty power that God has for us followers.

EPHESIANS 1:19 CEV

Spiritual Heroes

Who's your spiritual hero? Perhaps Mother Teresa's name comes to mind. Her tireless work among the poor in India earned her worldwide admiration. Or you might be thinking of Billy Graham. He spent a lifetime motivating believers to make God real and visible in their lives. Or maybe there's someone in your family or community whose peace, joy, and purpose have inspired you to desire that same peace, joy, and purpose for yourself.

But then you realize you lack the ability, experience, opportunity, or heartfelt calling to do what this person is doing. Does that mean God has given you nothing to do? Certainly not. It means only that He has blessed you with different spiritual gifts and that He intends you to start using them right where you are, because they are needed. No matter how noteworthy someone else's work appears, or how much acclaim it receives, you have your own God-given work to do, and it is as important in His eyes as anyone else's.

Praise and thank God for your spiritual heroes. Let them

inspire and motivate you not to long for their position and influence, but to imitate their willingness to give their time and talents to change things for the better. God doesn't need you to be a clone of someone else, but to become more and more the unique individual He has made you, joyfully living the God-blessed life He has planned for you.

There are different kinds of spiritual gifts, but the same Spirit is the source of them all.

1 CORINTHIANS 12:4 NLT

Genuine Growth

Perhaps you've heard the quip: A journey of a thousand miles begins with someone saying, "I know a shortcut!" While on the road, you might even have tried a few shortcuts yourself, only to find that the route you were sure went straight through to your destination didn't, but instead wound around for miles.

In our spiritual life, trying to take a shortcut yields no better results. Think of it this way: we would save time if, say, we could eat our week's meals all in one afternoon and be done with it, but we wouldn't remain healthy for long. That shortcut just won't work! Neither will a shortcut to sound spiritual health. There's no way to spiritual wisdom and maturity except through day-to-day living, God-centered thinking, and real-life experience.

God works through who we are and where we are. Our daily circumstances are what He uses to test our faith and give us opportunities to practice being loving, forgiving, patient, and kind in observable, practical ways. Suppose our quiet time with God has opened our eyes to the importance of sharing with others, but until we're around others and share our attention and resources with them, our insight remains simply a pious thought.

God has put you on the road to eternal life with Him in heaven. With His Spirit doing the steering, you will make progress every day toward spiritual maturity. You aren't in the same place you were yesterday, and you won't be where you are today a week from now. Be patient with yourself! There are no shortcuts on this road because lasting, genuine, God-given growth happens slowly, quietly, and without fail every step along the way.

Grow in the grace and knowledge of our Lord and Savior Jesus Christ.

2 PETER 3:18 ESV

Real-Life Holiness

While inexcusable behavior of others annoys us, it's our own inexcusable behavior that can cause us the most distress. Beyond the unfortunate incident itself, we live with the anger that brought on our regrettable outburst; the malice that spawned our unkind remark; the discouragement that preceded our decision to quit. It's far easier to forgive others their imperfections than it is to forgive ourselves for not being the angelic people we would like to be!

You've heard it said that forgiveness is more for the person offering forgiveness than for the one receiving it. You know that by forgiving, you're letting go of anger and bitterness, as well as a desire for revenge that can so readily darken the heart. Even if the other person refuses your forgiveness, or circumstances make it impossible to speak to the person, your act of forgiving allows you to go forward, freed from a terrible burden.

Have you offered forgiveness to yourself, though? Complete forgiveness, as you would extend to a close friend who has hurt you? Given to yourself as well as to others, forgiveness prepares your heart for the transforming work of the Holy Spirit as He nurtures seeds of patience, humility, and spiritual understanding within you. Forgiveness equips you to learn from what happened in the past and then let go of it and look to the future with wiser, more experienced eyes.

God has forgiven you completely. Now forgive yourself. Allow His Spirit to lead you into visible, real-life holiness in His own way and in His own time. Remain with Him because no one has the power to be holy apart from God, who is holy.

As far as the east is from the west, so far has he removed our transgressions from us.

PSALM 103:12 NIV

15

Here and Now

We cherish "someday" dreams. Our fantasies find us standing on the deck of a cruise ship headed for exotic destinations; owning the perfect home; enjoying active and healthy retirement years. "Someday!" we say, while adding, "God willing." Because no matter how carefully we plan, we don't know what the future may bring. We're both wise and realistic to put "someday" hopes in God's hands.

Putting today in His hands is different, though. If we're unable to do everything we plan—we're stuck in a traffic jam due to a collision a few blocks ahead, or we're sitting in the doctor's waiting room long past our appointment time—we're upset and angry. It doesn't cross our minds that perhaps our plans were not in sync with God's plans. While most of us accept the fact that one of our "someday" dreams might not come true, we're distraught when something we want to do today has to be delayed or put off until tomorrow.

Certainly, planning our day and making a God-pleasing, productive use of time is the smart and responsible thing to do. Yet today's plans, like tomorrow's, are subject to God's will and guidance. Who's to say that a traffic jam isn't a God-sent invitation to pray for those involved in an accident? Or our time in the waiting room a chance to encourage another patient dealing with a health issue ten times more serious than our own?

God knows your time is valuable—He gave it to you! But remember, just as your future rests in His hands, so does your present. If today doesn't go according to your plan, ask God about His plans. You never know what opportunity the moment may hold.

*What you ought to say is,
"If the Lord wants us to, we will
live and do this or that."*

JAMES 4:15 NLT

17

Enjoy Life

Some see God as a stern old gent, forever demanding us to do things we don't want to do. We want to free ourselves from His rules so we can enjoy life.

Yet flouting God's rules brings not freedom, but bondage—bondage to the tyranny of limited human reason and changeable personal feelings. Suppose we take lightly God's rule about loving our neighbor as ourselves. Then, when tempted to hate someone who offends us or envy the person who outshines us, we give in. Now chains of our own making hold us tight, and we're imprisoned by malice, vengeance, and discontent.

Or suppose we agree, in general, that stealing is wrong. But then we're in a job where we have access to the company's funds. We're running short on money this month, and it occurs to us that no one will know if we were to take a little here, a little there. So now we're burdened not only with the fear that someone might discover our theft, but a nagging conscience to boot!

In contrast, we can rest at complete ease under the protection of God's rules. Our loving creator has given them to us to keep us from the pitfalls of shortsighted reasoning, situational ethics, and our own impulsive acts. By obeying His commandments, we're allowing Him to give us true and lasting freedom.

If you struggle with one of God's rules, why not talk to Him about it? Pour out your thoughts, and then let Him talk to you in the words of scripture and through the voice of mature Christian friends and advisers. Free yourself to really enjoy your life.

"You shall walk after the LORD your God and fear him and keep his commandments and obey his voice."

DEUTERONOMY 13:4 ESV

Cry Out!

If you have ever taken care of a baby, you know all too well that babies can't do anything on their own. When they need food, or warmth, or comfort, they simply yell! That's all it takes for loving hands to pick them up, caring hands to give them food, and tender arms to enfold them. All this takes place, even though babies contribute no income to the household (just the opposite, as any parent will tell you) or do anything in exchange for what's done for them.

As adults, however, we're often stubbornly reluctant to let others do things for us. We might not want to feel obligated; we believe we don't deserve it; or we're reluctant to admit we can't help ourselves. It's not uncommon for someone to struggle for years rather than ask for assistance.

This is true in the spiritual life too. We're uncomfortable going to our heavenly Father for all sorts of reasons! Is there any way we can return the favor? No. Have we done enough to deserve His attention? No. Do we like admitting we aren't all-powerful, all-knowing, all-competent? No, no, and no!

Yet to God, we are like infants, reliant on Him to initiate, maintain, and nurture our growth and our relationship with Him.

God comes to you with love, compassion, and tenderness not because of who you are, but because of who He is. Without ever being able to earn a place with God or repay Him for His kindness, you are of immeasurable worth in His eyes. Cry out to Him! That's all it takes for Him to bend down, pick you up, and hold you close to His heart.

God is love.

1 JOHN 4:8 NIV

Really True

You've probably heard the warning: If something sounds too good to be true, it probably is. In God's world, though, things are different. When He gives you a gift, there are no strings attached. When He says it's free, it's free.

God offers love, attention, forgiveness, compassion, and eternal life with Him free of charge. Truly, there's no way we could pay for what God gives because everything we possess is from Him. It's as if a wealthy donor handed a million dollars to a poor family. Their sole healthy and productive response would be to love, thank, and respect their generous benefactor and honor him by using what they had received in a way that would please him.

On a grander scale, God is your generous benefactor. His plan of forgiveness and salvation for the whole world includes you. Jesus willingly came into the world to fulfill what His heavenly Father promised, suffer and die for all your sins, and rise again so you could know for sure that He has power over death. All this affects you! God's gift to you is Jesus, and He pours on you riches not even millions of dollars can buy—the comfort of His presence. Freedom from guilt. The assurance of a relationship with Him. Hope in the face of death.

Too good to be true? When God is the giver, it's true. Receive faith in Him with open arms and a grateful heart. Possess it in joy. Share it with delight.

God's gift is real life, eternal life, delivered by Jesus, our Master.

ROMANS 6:23 MSG

Hopes and Dreams

Like many girls who grew up in the 1950s, Janet dreamed of marrying a handsome man, having two or three children, and being a stay-at-home mom in a safe, quiet neighborhood like the one she knew. She prayed that God would make her dream come true, certain that her future happiness depended on God's yes.

But things did not turn out Janet's way. No Prince Charming crossed her path, and there were no children and no home of her own on a leafy suburban street. So had God not heard Janet's innocent pleadings? Yes, He certainly had. But He said, *"Please wait, My beloved child, because I have something else in mind for you, something you can't even imagine yet. You will find great happiness and complete fulfillment. Trust Me on this one!"*

As Janet grew in spiritual knowledge and gradually yielded herself to God's guidance, she realized that God indeed had a very special plan for her, one just right for her talents, interests, and abilities. As she focused her attention on her real-life circumstances, her childhood imaginings faded in importance, and she appreciated more and more her God-blessed reality. What He promised happened, and today her joy is complete.

Do you feel cheated because something you have desperately wanted is not yours? Then learn from Janet and countless others like her. Willingly release your hopes, dreams, and desires to God, trusting Him to know what will bring you happiness. Put your life in His hands, and then open your arms wide to receive His blessings. Will His blessings look like what you have always pictured? Maybe, maybe not. Either way, embrace what God, in His goodness, has given to you. Gladly throw yourself into today's circumstances because they are stepping-stones on your path to lasting joy.

"Test me in this and see if I don't open up heaven itself to you and pour out blessings beyond your wildest dreams."

MALACHI 3:10 MSG

The Best

Maybe you have asked this question: "If God loves us, then why does He allow pain, sickness, famine, wars, loss. . . ?" The list could go on forever! Truly, there's no shortage of woes in the world to bring us to our knees in tears.

While our loving Father in heaven is not the author of evil, He permits it. He has not chosen to answer all the questions we have concerning it, but He has given us everything we need to know about how to handle it. His Son Jesus willingly submitted Himself to a torturous death, experiencing pain and suffering firsthand. His resurrection from the tomb reveals, without doubt, God's power over evil. In our own pain and suffering, we can look to Jesus, who understands, sympathizes, and enfolds us in His strength and comfort.

Have you ever seen an artist take something ugly and create a meaningful piece of art out of it—even a beautiful one? That's similar to the way God works. Just as God brought a glorious resurrection out of a foul death, He continues to bring good out of bad. Amid the ugliness of evil, you have seen people act bravely and selflessly. Through the struggles you face, you become stronger, more insightful, and more able to encourage others.

You probably can think of a specific instance in your own life where a blessing came as a result of an unfortunate, even calamitous, event. Know, then, that any misfortune you go through will yield something good, true, and positive. Why? Because God loves you, and He gives you His best.

We know that in all things
God works for the good of
those who love him.

ROMANS 8:28 NIV

Love Received

If you know others love you, give thanks for such a magnificent gift—both their love and your realization of it. All you have to do, then, to glimpse God's love is to magnify their love millions and millions of times—and you still won't reach the limit of His feelings for you!

Yet far too many people have trouble believing that God loves them to any degree. The unloving ways of others or their own emotional shortcomings have convinced them that they are unworthy of love, and so they cannot believe they are loved by anyone, including God. For a heart set hard against love, love cannot enter.

On receptive as well as unreceptive hearts, toward the loving and unloving person, God continues to shower His love. The question of worthiness doesn't enter the picture because we are all unworthy of His love; yet the gift of His love is always there for us. We're incapable of experiencing it and responding to it, though, unless the Holy Spirit gives us the power to believe it's truly ours to possess.

Today, ask His Spirit to show you the ways of divine love. If you are blessed to know what earthly love is like, now is your chance to experience heavenly love. If you have found little love from the hearts of others, prepare to receive boundless love from the heart of God. Either way, His love is the same. It's unconditional, faithful, complete, and eternal. "Thank You, God," is all it takes to let Him know that you've received the gift He has for you.

"I have loved you with an everlasting love; therefore I have continued my faithfulness to you."

JEREMIAH 31:3 ESV

Leap of Faith

"Leap of faith" is the term many use to describe belief in God. The phrase aptly illustrates how it feels to us when we cast aside our reason, senses, and feelings, and simply say, "Yes, Lord; I believe!"

Over the millennia of recorded human thought, no theologian has been able to explain God in the same way horticulturalists can explain the composition of soil or how grass grows. You can't prove God exists in the same way you can prove that kerosene catches fire if you light a match to it. No one can!

Your senses rely on physical sight, hearing, and touch to learn about the world, but God comes to you through your spiritual senses. You're hardwired to wonder where you came from, why you're here, and what will happen at the time of death. Thoughts like these stir the soul, enlivening your spiritual senses, and now God's Spirit has a chance to move. He draws you to perceive that you're more than a physical body, and He is more than anything you can completely fathom.

When you consciously and deliberately take a leap of faith, it's as if you're saying to God, "Okay, I give up trying to use the scientific method to understand You. Reveal Yourself to me however You see fit." Now your heart and mind are open, and the Holy Spirit can really get to work! Though you might think you're giving up hope of knowing anything about Him, the opposite is true. The more you let God be God in your life, the more attuned your spiritual senses become to His presence and the more confidently you will believe in Him.

Faith holds on, even when physical senses fail. It's the answer that fills your soul, calms your fears, expands your insight, and deepens your appreciation of life. It's faith, and faith alone, that God asks of you. How do you answer Him?

Faith makes us sure of what we
hope for and gives us proof
of what we cannot see.

HEBREWS 11:1 CEV

Why Wait?

In movies, the hardened criminal's deathbed confession allows the priest to absolve him of his sins and convey the comforting promise of eternal life. In the real world too, a sincere confession at the end of life—no matter how that life has been lived—invites God's forgiveness and opens the soul to heaven's bliss. But why wait so long for the peace and joy that confession brings?

Putting off confession now is like relegating ourselves to a starvation diet with the intention of enjoying the satisfaction of a full meal five minutes before we die. That's certainly far from God's will for us. Instead, He would have us turn to Him in genuine repentance and confession every day so that He can nourish us with a continuing feast of spiritual blessings.

The assurance of God's forgiveness frees us from guilt that shadows our thoughts and lurks in the secret recesses of our hearts. It allows Him to feed us with peace of mind and a deep sense of inner rest and well-being. Confession also helps us see ourselves for who we are—individuals greatly in need of God's power to make positive changes in our lives. Every God-authored change brings increased happiness, more fulfillment, and greater joy. Why would we want to wait until some undetermined future time for these gifts?

Certainly, knowing you will be forgiven and received into heaven when your own time comes removes any dread of death. Happiness while you're living, however, lies in knowing you can receive forgiveness today. Right now, wherever you are. Why put off your heart-to-heart talk with your forgiving and compassionate God?

If we admit our sins—make a clean breast of them—he won't let us down; he'll be true to himself. He'll forgive our sins and purge us of all wrongdoing.

1 JOHN 1:9 MSG

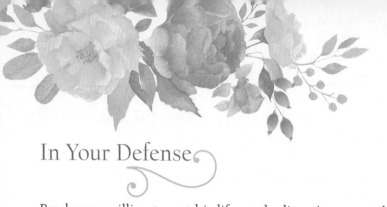

In Your Defense

Brody was willing to put his life on the line. As soon as he finished high school, he applied for a law-enforcement job. After training as a patrol officer, Brody asked to be assigned to one of the most dangerous districts in the city. When asked why, he said, "It's for the sake of the kids growing up there. I'm going there to protect them. I love those guys, and I'll give my life for them, if that's what it takes."

Sadly, Brody's life is what it took. In defending a group of kids playing in the park, he was fatally shot by a neighborhood gang member. But Brody's story doesn't end there. The young officer's willingness to give up his life rather than allow evil to have its way made an indelible impression on each of the kids. They never forgot, and if later you were to ask what made them choose to join the police force, enlist in the army, enter law school, major in education, train as a paramedic, you would hear one word: *Brody*.

Jesus, God's Son, came to earth in human form for one reason: us. Just as many among us are willing to die in defense of our country, our community, our family, Jesus was willing to die for us. He refused to leave us defenseless against the forces that would take us away from God's presence. In His resurrection, Jesus reminds us that He still lives, still loves us, and still is there to help us become like Him in thought, word, and action.

Now when someone asks what motivates you to follow God's way, you have your one-word answer: *Jesus*.

"I am the good shepherd.
The good shepherd sacrifices
his life for the sheep."

JOHN 10:11 NLT

Let Go

Some short mottos are long on wisdom, and the phrase "Let go and let God" is one of them. There are times when you must do that or flail around until you're completely exhausted. And to what purpose? At the end of mind-wrenching struggle, never-ending worry, and constant stress, what do you have? More struggle, worry, and stress!

You might be able to recall a time when a particular problem haunted you all day long. Any solution you came up with only brought with it another problem, perhaps one worse than the first. By evening, you vowed to put the issue aside and aim for a good night's sleep. "I'll tackle it in the morning," you promised yourself. When you woke in the morning, you were astonished to realize that a simple, clear, and obvious solution was right there for the taking.

That's what happens when you turn things over to God. After you've done everything you can, give the problem over to God. Don't worry about it any longer, but put it in His hands in confidence because He can do what you cannot.

He might give you the knowledge and resources it takes to solve or manage the problem, or take care of it in a way you could have never expected.

There's an added bonus when you "let go and let God" too. Because you're not swathed in worry, you're free to relax and watch His divine wisdom at work!

Give your burdens to the LORD,
and he will take care of you.

PSALM 55:22 NLT

Commitment in Action

The young piano student is determined to make it to the concert hall. Imagine the thoughts that go through her mind, though, as she looks out of the window on a sunny afternoon and sees the neighborhood kids playing a pickup game of softball in the field across the street. Is she tempted to forgo the day's practice session and join the game? The choice she makes tells us more about her level of commitment than any words could say.

Think of the daily effort and long-term commitment it takes to accomplish anything worthwhile! Certainly, growth in spiritual knowledge and holy living is no exception because the temptation to do something else presents itself daily. During the time we set aside in the morning for reflecting on God's Word, thoughts of all our daily to-dos urge us to get up and get started. Though we promise ourselves we'll spend a few minutes in prayer before bedtime, sleep presses hard on us, reminding us how early the alarm clock will ring.

Here are a couple of other common temptations. After the excitement of embracing a relationship with God, we lose our initial enthusiasm. (Isn't that often the case with any new venture we take up?) Also, our worries and problems can take over our thoughts, leaving no space for thoughts of God. Or, experiencing what the mystics of old called "spiritual dryness," we give up our spiritual quest altogether.

Does temptation lure you? That's a clear sign you're making progress because only someone already on the journey can be tempted away from it. Now look at your actions. If they show anything less than true commitment, ask God to grant you the strength and power to make the right choice.

"Blessed are those who hunger and thirst for righteousness, for they shall be satisfied."

MATTHEW 5:6 ESV

God-Sight

Although we can't see air, we know it's around us. Air is in every breath we take, and it's essential to life. We can't see carbon monoxide, either, yet a high concentration of the invisible gas causes death. Neither can we see gravity, yet its force affects everything we do. Just because our eyes can't perceive it doesn't mean it doesn't exist!

With this in mind, let's turn our thoughts to our heavenly Father. See Him, as we would the face of a friend? Touch His hand? Brush against His arm? No; yet He is as real as the air we breathe. Certainly, God has the power to make Himself visible to us, but that's not the way He works among us. Though He is present, we cannot perceive Him with our physical senses as we would an object or another person.

Why not? Perhaps it's our human tendency not to look past physical appearance. Our unseen God compels us to search for Him in heart and mind, and in the Bible, where He most distinctly reveals Himself. Or perhaps He wants no one to imagine that He favors one physical place over another and that we must ourselves make the journey to visit Him. Just the opposite! His Holy Spirit makes the journey to visit us, wherever we happen to be.

How do you picture your heavenly Father? Yet all human conceptions of Him fall far short of who He really is—your all-powerful and ever-present God who loves you, cares for you, and hears you each time you come to Him in prayer.

"God is sheer being itself—Spirit."

JOHN 4:24 MSG

Faith Alone

Imagine meeting a woman who tells you this: "My day is chock-full of tasks. Although they're useless tasks and I'll end up exhausted at the end of the day, I'm going to do them anyway." Truly, you would wonder about her sanity!

When we attempt to earn our salvation, however, we're behaving like this woman. Say we spend every day doing good things, hoping to win points from God. Useless! Though we may receive heartfelt thanks from the people, we've done nothing to ensure our salvation. At day's end, we'll feel utterly depleted and left wondering whether or not we've done enough to please Him. Why? Because we don't have the power to bring about eternal life for ourselves. Only Jesus, God's Son, could—and He did.

No matter how saintly we are, we still aren't perfect. Struggles, stumbles, and temptations will nip at our heels throughout our earthly walk. Imperfect, we cannot stand in God's divine presence, any more than a speck of dirt can settle in a glass of pure water without turning the water impure. So here's what Jesus, holy and perfect, came to do: earn our place in front of God through His life, death, and resurrection.

Just as you rely on Jesus' work for your salvation, depend on His Spirit to give you the faith—the power—to believe in what He has done for you. Now let your joy and gratitude motivate the many kindnesses you do, and you will not only please others but God as well.

You have never seen Jesus, and you don't see him now. But still you love him and have faith in him, and no words can tell how glad and happy you are to be saved.

1 PETER 1:8–9 CEV

It's a Promise

In the Bible, God has made many promises to us. Some of them already have been fulfilled, like His promise to send a Savior to defeat the power of sin over us. Jesus, our Savior, has sacrificed Himself for our sins and has risen from the tomb in victory over eternal death. Other promises, like His promise to come again at the end of time, have yet to be fulfilled. And then there are His ongoing promises, like His promise to say yes to our prayers.

If we earnestly pray for something and don't receive it, however, we start doubting this promise. If He means what He said, then why don't we get everything we ask for? It's not as if we're asking for mean or wicked things, is it? We pray for, perhaps, better health, a higher standard of living, a friend's release from illness, a job for our out-of-work relative, and, by the way, an end to famine and world peace. So where's His yes? Is He even listening?

God promises to hear all prayer spoken in faith in the saving work of Jesus Christ. That's because Jesus is the one who made a relationship between you and God the Father possible. So rest assured He listens when you bring Him your needs, requests, and desires, and He says yes. Yes, not necessarily to the specific things you've asked for, but exactly what you would have asked for if you possessed His infinite wisdom and knowledge. You may not receive your yes in the form you expect, but you will receive it.

Throughout the history of humankind, God has kept His promises; He still keeps them today. Pray in complete faith that He says yes to all that you ask, according to His will and His love for you.

"You may ask me for anything in my name, and I will do it."

JOHN 14:14 NIV

100 Percent

Without trust in each other, no one could relax for a moment! Indeed, we put our trust in others every day. We trust drivers to obey traffic signals; trust builders to erect sturdy structures; trust grocers to sell safe food; trust the people around us to do what they say they're going to do.

But life soon teaches us not to trust 100 percent. Not all drivers heed traffic lights, and not all workers are honest. Some sellers will try to cut corners, and some people will let us down. Sometimes we ourselves fail to honor the trust a person has placed in us. As we learn the ways of the world, we balance the necessity of trusting others so we can live together in community with good sense stemming from practical experience.

When our hard-earned lesson not to trust unwisely extends to God, we need to remind ourselves of an inescapable fact: we are human, and God is God. While we fall short of perfection, God is perfection itself. Though we don't always keep our word, God keeps His, down to the letter. If we read God's biblical promises in context, grasp their clearest meaning, we can put 100 percent of our trust in them.

Trust God without reservation. The one who created you will take care of you, and the one who sent His Son to redeem you will not cast you off. His Holy Spirit, who is working to strengthen your faith right now, will never let you down. Give 100 percent of your trust to the one who gives you 100 percent of His love.

With all your heart you must trust the LORD and not your own judgment.

PROVERBS 3:5 CEV

Thy Will Be Done

Have you ever worked with a person who micromanages? If you have, you know what it's like to have someone constantly looking over your shoulder to see if you're doing your job the right way (that is, the precise way the micromanager believes it should be done). For every move you make, he or she has a comment or criticism, a prompt or suggestion. Clearly, this micromanager puts no faith in your skill, knowledge, or competency.

There are few among us who have never tried to micromanage God. Though we tell Him our desires and say, "Thy will be done," we immediately start thinking to ourselves exactly how God should answer our prayer. We look for a particular result, or at least a special sign, and when we don't see it, we're back at God's side, prodding Him to get busy, to make things work out, to do it *now*, and to do it *our* way.

If we believe God is capable of giving us what we need, why can't we see that He's doing exactly that? If we admit our heavenly Father wants only the best for us, why do we attempt to direct His hands? If we acknowledge He knows more than we do, why do we expect Him to follow our instructions?

If you recognize yourself as one of your heavenly Father's many micromanagers, it's time to step back. When you pray, let "Thy will be done" become your words of complete trust in your all-powerful, all-wise, and fully competent God.

"I want your will to be done, not mine."

LUKE 22:42 NLT

To This Day

As he wakes on the morning of his seventieth birthday, Bill reflects on his life. He recalls with tenderness his strict but loving parents; his pretty high school sweetheart who waited for him to return from the war; their happy marriage, their three healthy children, his fulfilling career and adequately funded retirement. Sure, there were some significant challenges along the way. "Thank God," he whispers to himself, "I didn't know about them ahead of time! I wouldn't have believed myself able to go on—but when the time came to handle it, I did. Thank You, Lord!" Yes, Bill has to admit that he has had a good life.

But what about the future? Several of his coworkers and friends have passed away within the past five years. Others are dealing with ongoing health problems, including his beloved wife. While Bill remains active now, images of what may lie ahead darken his thoughts. Quite unlike himself, he feels little desire even to get out of bed.

The morning brightens as he dozes, and somewhere in

his wandering thoughts a whisper embraces him as a soft, soothing, warming ray of sunshine: *"I have brought you to this day. I have guided, sustained, strengthened, and comforted you to this day, and I have led you through every difficulty to this day. Why, then, would I, the one who has seen you through seven decades, not see you through the future, whatever it might bring?"*

God has seen you through to this day. Will He suddenly abandon you? Certainly not! God is faithful at every stage, at every age, at every season of your life.

*Don't throw me aside when
I am old; don't desert me
when my strength is gone.*

PSALM 71:9 CEV

Practice Trust

"Practice makes perfect," it's said. While reaching perfection might be a stretch, practice certainly enables us to do things better. Playing golf takes practice. Baking a cake, sewing a dress, or building a boat in a bottle—these all take practice before what we're doing feels familiar and comfortable.

Inner habits take practice too. Anything we might want to cultivate within ourselves—joy, gratitude, trust, compassion—we have to practice. While some people may appear naturally joyful, for instance, it's quite probable that their joy stems from a decision to be a joyful person. When they start feeling down in the dumps, they seize the opportunity to practice joy. They might listen to music that lifts their mood, start a list of things they're thankful for, or consciously greet others with a friendly nod and warm smile. With practice, they feel happy, and they're soon known as joyful, optimistic, and great-to-be-around people!

Trust is no different. If you have trouble trusting God, decide to start practicing. Do you trust Him to continue loving you? Do you trust Him to send His Spirit into your heart? Do you trust Him to guide you today? Do you trust Him to be there for you tomorrow? Whenever one of these questions enters your thoughts, practice trust in that specific instance, and soon placing your trust in God will feel like the obvious and natural thing to do. While practice might not bring perfection, it will bring you the peace of mind that those who trust in God enjoy.

In him our hearts rejoice, for we trust in his holy name.

PSALM 33:21 NIV

Feelings for You

Songwriters would soon be out of business if there were no emotion called love! Even if love has never swept us off our feet, we can imagine the glorious excitement of romance. We can still smile and understand because love, in its many forms, draws us close to others. It sparks interest in life, forges bonds between people, and allows us a glimpse of God's compassionate feelings toward us.

Our emotions are God's gifts to us. Joy, wonder, desire, elation, and fondness weave through our years like threads of gold. Even emotions like anger, grief, and regret enhance our lives when they spur us to productive action, such as to fight injustice, honor the dead, and right a wrong.

But emotions, like all God's gifts, can be misused and misapplied. If you were to allow "feeling happy" to become your main goal, you'd soon be shifting from one thing to another in search of happiness, yet nothing would give you lasting pleasure. Were desire to take precedence in your life, you would never be able to experience the gifts of contentment and gratitude for what you have. Allow anger to gain control, and you would find it impossible to forge healthy relationships and enjoy a peaceful and stable life.

Embrace your emotions, for they are truly God's gifts to you. Rejoice that you're able to feel empathy, affection, tenderness, compassion, ambition, and caring. Let songwriters continue praising love and lovers alike! But, with the help and power of His Spirit, take charge of your feelings. If God's commandments would not lead you there, don't let your emotions take you there.

Let your reasonableness be known to everyone.

PHILIPPIANS 4:5 ESV

Rule of Faith

At times, we're called upon to defend our faith in God's authority. Skeptics question why God would say something is wrong when it's what ordinary people are doing with no obvious ill effect. They might argue that sacrificing personal pleasure for the sake of obedience to God's commandments is old-fashioned and a hindrance to self-realization. Sometimes the skeptic's voice is none other than our own.

The skeptic within us may argue in favor of the Bible's timeless wisdom concerning the human condition, yet note that other writings, both sacred and secular, offer equally insightful statements. Our inner skeptic may revere Jesus as a remarkable teacher, but if a teacher is all He means to us, we'll feel free to tweak His words so they fit easily into our reasoning and wants in life.

Only if we're willing to accept the Bible as God's words to us will we take what it says seriously. Only if we're willing to embrace Jesus as our living Lord will we diligently apply His teaching to our daily thoughts, actions, words, and decisions. When we do, we're going against what many people think and what they do. Some will scoff, some will insult us, some will take us to task. And yes, we might even come up with a few uncomfortable comments ourselves.

It comes down to this: you believe what He says, or you don't. God invites you to let His Spirit silence the questions within and strengthen your resolve to live according to His Word. He helps you respond to the voices of others, and to the skeptic within, with wisdom and understanding, kindness and love. His presence is your best and truest defense.

We will speak the truth in love, growing in every way more and more like Christ.

EPHESIANS 4:15 NLT

Keep Going

Bad habits are hard to break! Even though we know what we're doing is wrong, we do it anyway. If we're successful in stopping, relapses undo hard-earned progress, and we have to start all over again. How much easier to give up and give in! We justify our defeat by thinking, *Well, I'm only human*, or *There are other sins worse than this one*.

Seemingly unconquerable habits, however, can be a blessing in disguise. First, we discover that a pattern of wrongdoing isn't changed simply by making a personal resolution. Victory takes God's power within us initiating repentance, instituting change, and igniting resolve. Second, our recognition of personal sin draws us to humbly confess our faults and receive God's forgiveness, deepening our appreciation for His mercy.

Third, acknowledging our own weaknesses renders us more tolerant of the weaknesses of others. We're compelled to forgive them their shortcomings, as our heavenly Father has forgiven ours. Our struggle with our own sins enables us to empathize with the struggles of others. We know it's not easy to overcome a bad habit, to replace old ways of doing things for new, and effect lasting change.

If there is a particular sin that burdens you, take it to your Lord in prayer. Ask Him to forgive you and free you from its grip. Let Him show you little ways you can avoid it, then big ways, and bigger ways. If you fall a few steps back occasionally, go forward again with your Lord at your side. Keep going forward!

What I don't understand about myself is that I decide one way, but then I act another, doing things I absolutely despise.

ROMANS 7:15 MSG

Pleased to Please

Sometimes you meet someone and it's as if you had known each other for a lifetime. That's the way it was when Paula first saw Teri sitting by herself at a club meeting. Paula sat down next to her, introduced herself, and the two fell into easy conversation.

Though they shared many interests, they differed in one: Paula was an expert cook and adventurous eater, while Teri had serious digestive problems and her menu was limited. When friends invited her to a home-cooked dinner, Teri never accepted their invitations because she didn't like being a burden and asking hosts to accommodate her restricted diet.

But Paula didn't need to be asked. She did the asking, researched recipes, and discovered many she had never fixed before that would allow her to provide a delightful meal for her friend to enjoy. Paula wasn't required, but she chose to bypass tried-and-true dishes in favor of unfamiliar ones, all to please her friend.

Certainly no one could reasonably accuse Paula of not possessing a will of her own. Of course she did, but she chose to serve Teri instead and put affection for her friend first and her personal inclinations second. It's what people do when a relationship means something to them.

Your relationship with God is no different. If you wanted something and God said no, would you risk your friendship with Him to get it? If you knew your words or actions went against His guidelines, would you persist? If you realized a particular attitude dampened your appreciation of His gifts, would you let it continue?

He is your friend who chooses the best for you. How are you that kind of friend to Him?

"If you love me, you will keep my commandments."

John 14:15 esv

Good Purpose

God's will for His people is that we believe in His Son Jesus and live according to His commandments. This is clearly taught in the Bible, and it applies to all of us. In addition, He has a specific purpose for individual believers, and He calls each of us by name. In answering His call, we discover personal fulfillment and lasting joy.

For some, God's call is plain from an early age. You've likely heard many accomplished people say, "I've always known I wanted to be a missionary," or "From the day my aunt took me to the hospital where she worked, I wanted to be a doctor." But most of us aren't sure of our path so young, and we aren't aware of a unique calling. We pursue what we suppose is a fairly ordinary course of life, later wondering if God ever meant us for any specific purpose, and if so, what is it?

You can determine your calling simply by observing who you are and where you are. If you're a parent, guardian, or caregiver, you are called to extend God's caring and compassion to others. If you're in the workplace, you are called to be God's light among people who may not know His love for them. If you volunteer, you are called to give selflessly and generously in visible, practical ways.

What are your responsibilities right now? What does His Spirit prompt you to do, or where does He urge you to go? Look and see your life through His eyes, and you will know His good, gracious, and fulfilling plan and purpose for you.

It is God who works in you to will and to act in order to fulfill his good purpose.

PHILIPPIANS 2:13 NIV

The Real Reason

Every morning, Christina began her shift at the turnpike tollbooth. At first, she found it lonely and boring; she dreamed of something better, more exciting and prestigious.

One cold, snowy morning, when she was deep in her imaginings, a car slowly pulled up and the window rolled down. "It's slippery in places," the young driver said, clearly shaken, as she handed Christina a dollar bill. "I'm so glad to see someone." Christina smiled, reassured the girl, advised her to be careful. Touched by the girl's need, Christina whispered a prayer for her safety as her car pulled away. *Glad to see someone!* The words sang in her heart as her eyes fell on the photo she always carried with her. The smiling face of her three-year-old daughter looked back at her, the girl's blue eyes sparkling with joy. "I'm glad I'm here and I could pray for that young woman because that's what I would want someone to do for my daughter."

From that day forward, Christina had a smile and a greeting for every driver and found herself meeting people from all walks of life. Her work became rewarding because drivers appreciated her sunny attitude and told her so. Soon Christina could depend on meeting dozens of "regulars" throughout the workweek.

Whatever God's will is for you right now, you meet challenges. Perhaps you struggle with a certain aspect of your calling, or you're reluctant to accept a difficult part of it, or you wish He would ask you to do something else entirely. Lift the eyes of your soul to Him, and see the good you are doing; discover ways to reap its rewards. Then pour yourself into it with all your heart!

Work willingly at whatever you do, as though you were working for the Lord rather than for people.

Colossians 3:23 nlt

God's Gate

Imagine you're walking along the road and suddenly come upon an intersection. In one direction lies a street lined with everything your heart desires. If shopping's your pleasure, you're seeing the finest boutiques in the world, one after another. If you prefer serene arbors and shaded footpaths, you're gazing at the most beautiful garden imaginable.

In the other direction, you notice a narrow gate. Tall hedges prevent you from peeking beyond the gate, so you have no idea what's behind it. Yet you hear a tender voice coming from inside saying, *"My child, follow Me."* And the gate opens, inviting you to step inside.

If you put your faith in your own reasoning and judgment, you'll choose the first road. And why not? It's attractive and appealing, and you think you know what you're getting. But if you put your faith in God, He will call you to take the second road. Why? Because it shows you trust Him to know what you're getting.

Once through His gate, you'll discover a small path

marked not with hard pavement, but with the indelible footsteps of God. They wind through thorny places, but you hear Him say, *"Don't worry; I'll lift you up."* God's footsteps pass through dark places, and you hear Him say, *"Don't worry; I will comfort you."* They will take you to pleasant places, and you hear Him say, *"Receive My lasting joy."*

Look for God's footsteps, wherever you are today. Follow them, wherever they may lead.

I am the LORD, and I lead
you along the right path.

HOSEA 14:9 CEV

God's Footsteps

No one relishes criticism, but if you put God first in your life, you're bound to get your share of it. People might not tell you in so many words, but you'll see it in their faces when you pass on joining them at the gym on Sunday morning in favor of attending church. Or when you don't tell obscene stories, use curse words, or pass along gossip about others. Or when they see you share a generous portion of your time, abilities, and resources to help those less fortunate than yourself.

Not everyone follows God's rules, and many claim they don't even care about God's rules or His ways. So if you are walking with Him, don't expect applause from the sidelines. Don't look for unanimous approval, overwhelming acceptance, unconditional support, or ongoing encouragement. In fact, you can count yourself fortunate when all mockers do is ignore you rather than tell you face-to-face what they think!

Yet for all the verbal and nonverbal scorn that may come your way, your God-motivated choices stand as your best defense. Inner strength, peace of mind, spiritual insight, and evident integrity are life fulfilling; selfishness, pride, and pleasure seeking are not. With God, you gain strength, resilience, and wisdom that will see you through dark paths and tough times; but without Him, you are like a leaf in the wind, drifting this way and that, depending on the currents.

If you're wondering which way to turn today, look to God and His Word. Is there clear direction in scripture? Then go that way without hesitation! If there is not, pray for His Spirit's guidance. Either way, no matter what others may say or think, listen to Him.

If you're treated badly for good behavior and continue in spite of it to be a good servant, that is what counts with God.

1 PETER 2:20 MSG

God's Way

Anyone who strives to live according to God's will eventually faces this question: What exactly *is* God's will for me in this particular circumstance? The Bible tells us that God does not want us to cheat, steal, lie, or murder. But where does it tell us which job to take, where we should live, or whom to marry? Though the Bible is not specific on these personal decisions, it is not silent.

As you delve into God's Word and meditate on its meaning, you often will discover that certain verses spring to your attention—verses that apply to the question you're facing at the moment, or shed light on a decision you need to make. You may find in the Bible a principle pertaining to the issue in front of you, receiving the inner strength and confidence it takes to go forward boldly, thoughtfully, and prayerfully.

Then again, you might close the Bible, apparently with no more sense of direction than when you opened it. But keep looking and listening! Your real-life circumstances and your heartfelt, recurring feelings offer clues to God's next steps for you. Are there good things present that you can continue to strengthen with your time and attention? Are there things that need to be brought into harmony with God's good will, and what can you do to make that happen? What action would bring you closer to God? What action would share the reality of His love with others?

God wants you to know the joy of following Him, so He won't make it impossible for you to do so. Remain patient, and wait on His signs. Trust Him to show you your way in His way.

Teach me to do your will,
for you are my God.

PSALM 143:10 NIV

71

God's Word

Any religion's sacred writings contain verses that can be—and often are—taken out of context. The Bible is no different. Many Christian leaders, purporting to preach the Bible, highlight only the verses that serve their special interests or personal opinion. When they attract followers, a cult is born.

As individuals, we're not exempt from doing the same thing. Here's an example: Mary earnestly prays for more income so she can better feed her family, and she reads in the Bible God's promise to answer prayer. Then along comes a coworker who invites Mary, a bookkeeper, to join him in a plan to embezzle their employer. "That must be God's answer to my prayer!" Mary decides, and so agrees to go along with the crime.

Yet Mary has failed to remember that God forbids theft and fraudulent dealings. For that reason, His answer to Mary's prayer could not possibly have been her coworker's scheme. Had she considered God's Word in its entirety instead of choosing only what she wanted to hear, she would have made a wiser, God-pleasing choice.

Studying the entire Bible, preferably under the guidance of a mature, knowledgeable Christian, shields you from faulty theology and false conclusions. Follow clear teachings; where there are shadows, allow the Bible to shed light on them with other relevant passages. Most of all, know this: Bible study is a lifelong journey! Only God Himself knows it all.

Every part of Scripture is God-breathed and useful one way or another—showing us truth, exposing our rebellion, correcting our mistakes, training us to live God's way.

2 TIMOTHY 3:16 MSG

God's Gift

Whether you were raised in a Christian family or came to faith later in life, you no doubt have grappled with this question: How is Christianity different from other religions and belief systems? You find that other faiths and philosophies draw devoted adherents, same as Christianity. You might work or socialize with non-Christians and know for certain they are as honest, thoughtful, respectful, and spiritually minded as you are.

On the outside, devout people of goodwill throughout the world have much in common. They live quietly, take care of their own, uphold the law, resist injustice, help others, and encourage responsibility, stability, and faithfulness. Countless among them further enhance their community through their volunteer work, their godly influence, and their financial resources.

On the inside, however, there's a striking difference. Spiritually minded non-Christians (and misguided Christians) are motivated by hopes of winning God's favor, earning their salvation, or attaining a benefit of some kind, such as personal enlightenment or public recognition. All the while, however, there's the burden of wondering whether sufficient work has been done, or done well enough, to satisfy God.

God removes the burden of wondering from the Christian who accepts His grace with a heart of thanksgiving. It's by His grace that He loves, forgives, and saves—nothing else! So the Christian, motivated by the gift of His free, unearned, and unearnable grace, responds by living and acting according to His will.

Your heavenly Father invites you to let Him do for you what you cannot do, and that is take care of your soul's salvation. Let all your acts of kindness, compassion, selflessness, and tenderness be done not to gain, but because of, His great gift to you.

By grace you have been saved through faith. And this is not your own doing; it is the gift of God.

EPHESIANS 2:8 ESV

Tools for Living

If you're a woodworker, or sculptor, or quilter, or gardener, you know the value of having the right tool for the job at hand. Sure, you can make do with something else, but you are likely to find the task more difficult and the results unsatisfactory.

God has given you a range of "tools" to use as you progress through your life. Some are exterior, such as your natural capacities, as well as the skills you have learned, talents you have cultivated, and abilities you have developed. Others are interior. For example, you can think and reason, ponder and pray, and, with the presence of His Spirit in you, accept and believe His Word. He gives all these "tools" as blessings for you to use, but He cautions you to use the right one for the task in front of you.

Suppose you're confronted with a clear, yet personally troublesome, commandment in the Bible. Yes, you would use your ability to hear, read, and meditate on the point; but instead of going along with human judgment on the matter, you use the tool of faith, leading you to accept and obey this commandment. Or suppose you have a decision to make about, say, whom to marry. While the importance of your faith would prompt you to pick a godly person, you would also use your God-given ability to weigh other things, such as companionability, physical attraction, shared interests and goals, and personal preference.

For most anything you do, using the right tool is important. When it comes to avoiding life's pitfalls and possessing life's many gifts, it's essential!

Living wisely brings
pleasure to the sensible.

PROVERBS 10:23 NLT

Road Signs

Suppose you're taking a road trip across the country. You have thousands of miles to cover, and you plan to stop at certain rest areas, scenic spots, towns, and cities along the way. Now if you're driving along and not seeing the signs and landmarks you expected, wouldn't you begin to wonder if you're heading in the right direction?

Similarly, there are times when we have our sights set on a certain goal—it might be a particular job, certain position, or specific state in life. In our enthusiasm for our project, we become convinced that we are pursuing God's will for us. But the harder we work to get where we want to go, the more frustrated we become. Why? Because we're not seeing any obvious and objective signs of success, or even indications of modest progress.

This is a time for us to pause and reflect. While our goal might be God's will, are we going about it in His way and in His time? Then again, hard as it is, we may have to face the fact that we're not headed in the right direction at all.

Perhaps what we so earnestly desire would bring us neither happiness nor fulfillment (we don't know the future; God does). Maybe the place we're striving for belongs to someone else, and our real blessings lie in another place.

If you're met with frustration at every turn, take some time out to reflect on your destination and the way you're taking to get there. Ask God for a sign to help you discern His true will for you right now. He will give it! With the strength of His Spirit enabling you, express your willingness to follow Him, wherever He may lead.

"Why do you insist on going against the grain?"

Acts 26:14 MSG

Spiritually Mature

Many of us have fond memories of childhood—the parents we loved, the pets we adored, the friends we made, and the teachers whose patience, understanding, and encouragement helped us more than words could say. No matter how idyllic the time may have been, however, few of us would choose to remain a child or want to become a child again.

In our walk with God, however, we may find spiritual childhood a safe and consoling place to stay. We'll happily embrace a few simple Bible truths, such as God's presence and His love for us. As spiritual children, less comfortable topics like sin and repentance scare us. Though we're glad to come and worship the Babe of Bethlehem, we're reluctant to walk with Him to the cross of Calvary. While we rejoice at His resurrection, we avoid contemplating why He died in the first place.

Let us all open our arms wide to receive our heavenly Father's love for us! Let us depend on Him always for strength and guidance, as an innocent child would a loving parent.

But let us also grow in understanding, knowledge, and comprehension, and not stubbornly remain in spiritual kindergarten. Unless we mature spiritually, the questions, doubts, temptations, and trials of adulthood may crush a willfully weak and undeveloped faith.

If you are able and willing to delve deeper into spiritual matters, let the Spirit of God teach you. Some subjects might require effort and perseverance, but isn't that true of all learning? When you finally gain skill and expertise in a subject, don't you feel good? Now you're ready for the next lesson, and the one after that for a vital, growing, strong, vibrant, and mature faith!

People who live on milk are like babies who don't really know what is right.

HEBREWS 5:13 CEV

81

Love and Care

Is there someone special in your life? When you're apart, do you wonder what he or she is doing at this moment? If the person fell ill, would you offer comfort, even if it's at an inconvenient time for you? If you saw that person engaged in something dangerous, would you rush to intervene, even if he or she resisted your involvement?

When one of God's commandments infringes on what we're doing, we often respond with annoyance and defensiveness. We don't like being stopped in our tracks, bothered with divine advice, or hampered in our pursuit of "happiness." Yes, we want God to love us dearly, *and* we want Him to support all our plans. Impossible combination? Of course it is. With God as with ourselves, genuine love and active caring go hand in hand. One cannot exist without the other.

A guilty conscience isn't comfortable, but it's a sure sign of God's love for you. His Spirit whispers warnings in your heart because He is interested in your spiritual and physical well-being. A particular divine truth rushes to mind because what you're doing or contemplating goes against God's commandments. His love demands that He interfere, and rest assured, He will.

God grants you the ability to choose His way or follow your own. Yet even if you go your own way, His care for you never dims, and He remains waiting for you to return to Him. That's what love does. You know that, don't you? Perhaps you have waited—or are waiting—for someone you love to come back. The more you love, the more you care and the longer you'll wait.

When people do not accept divine guidance, they run wild. But whoever obeys the law is joyful.

PROVERBS 29:18 NLT

Nonstop Obedience

Katie was a ten-year-old in love with dance. She took lessons twice weekly, and she had dreams of becoming a professional ballerina. While her parents encouraged her, they never forced her to continue her lessons. As it happened, they never had to. Yes, sometimes Katie didn't particularly feel like going to class, but she went anyway. She knew if she wanted to reach the top of her chosen profession, she needed years of nonstop training.

In a way, God "trains" us toward obedience to His will and knowledge of His Word. On many occasions we might not particularly feel like following His lead, say, by making an effort to be kind and patient, or doing what we know is the God-pleasing thing to do. Yet the more we follow anyway, the more spiritually nimble we become; as nimble people, we're able to stretch further and further, accomplishing God's will with increasing strength, ease, and pleasure.

Obedience to God in practical, visible ways takes practice. Skip an opportunity to do His will, and you have lost a chance to flex your spiritual muscles. Willfully disobey once, and you will find obedience harder the next time, until, having missed so many "lessons," you no longer even want to obey!

Your nonstop, habitual obedience to God's will keeps you spiritually strong, nimble, and confident. But even if you stumble, do what Katie would do—get up and start again! It's the way to proficiency; it's the way to joy.

"Devote your heart and soul to seeking the LORD your God."

1 CHRONICLES 22:19 NIV

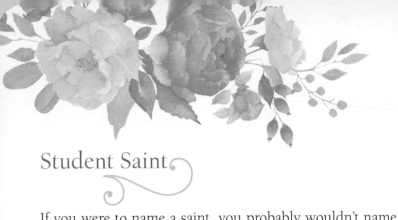

Student Saint

If you were to name a saint, you probably wouldn't name yourself. But a saint is what you are—a saint in the making as you grow closer to God and as your will and desires more closely reflect His.

You are also a saint right now because Jesus made you one. Since it's sin that bars you from sainthood, Jesus took all your sins upon Himself. As God, Jesus was the only one capable of such a sacrifice, and as Man, the only one able to atone for humanity's sins. His death paid the price, and His resurrection proved the point. Although you do wrong, you will not be condemned. Yes, you will sin this side of heaven, but heaven is assured. Jesus has bathed you in His perfection, wrapped you in His pure robes, and presents you as a saint to His heavenly Father.

Many of us, however, back away from the sainthood Jesus offers. Memories of past sins cause us to doubt that God could forgive us completely. Maybe He forgives other people and makes them saints, we think, but not us—not because of *that* sin we have committed. We've asked for forgiveness, but the moment we lay our sin down in front of Him, we snatch it up again and drag it around like a dirty rag.

Jesus offers forgiveness, and it is yours to take. Fill your heart with His forgiveness, and you will have no more room for guilt. No matter what the sin, or how many times you may have committed it, believe that Jesus has removed it. You can call yourself a saint because He does.

Sing praises to the LORD,
O you his saints, and give
thanks to his holy name.

PSALM 30:4 ESV

Without a Doubt

The further along we are in our relationship with God, the more strongly doubt attempts to undermine our faith and trust in Him. That's because we have begun to invest bigger portions of our efforts and resources in serving others, often at considerable sacrifice to ourselves. *Is it all worth it?* doubt whispers. We're now spending more of our time reading and meditating on His Word. When what it teaches clashes with popular standards or condemns our own behavior, doubt surfaces, suggesting that God's Word is not relevant to our lives.

Your doubts are not unusual, and they damage your relationship to God only if you let them pull you away from Him because you're relying on human reasoning and understanding. Instead, let each doubt you have prompt you to pray for strengthened faith and motivate you to dig deeper into God's Word. Let doubt compel you to look more closely at His work in your life and inspire you to walk in humble gratitude as His Spirit fills you with the assurance of His presence and His love for you.

"The people who have faith in me without seeing me are the ones who are really blessed!"

JOHN 20:29 CEV

Just Curious

Curious people are interesting people. They enthusiastically examine how things work, and they tirelessly probe for answers. It's almost assured that they'll have something new to say every time you see them!

Curiosity can enrich and enlarge your life, and also your spiritual experience. As you ask questions and receive answers, listen to how God works in the lives of others and find out more about what the Bible teaches. Your curiosity keeps your soul nourished and your knowledge growing. Curious about other religions? Learn about them! There's no other way you can compare and contrast Christianity with other belief systems unless you know something about them.

Yet temptation accompanies curiosity. You've heard it said that "curiosity killed the cat." Just as a cat, lured by a fluttering wing on a tree branch, climbs so high that it fears coming down again, curiosity can get us "treed" too. It happens when curiosity leads us into skepticism. We decide to stay perched above it all, neither believing nor disbelieving, but doubting everything. Though we imagine we're enjoying the elevation of a sophisticated position, we're simply closing our minds to any further pursuit of the spiritual life.

Perhaps there are scriptural and spiritual mysteries that you're curious about. What are they? Name them, and then prayerfully let your curiosity explore, examine, probe, and ponder them. You never know what truths God will make clear to you! But don't let temptation take your feet off the firm ground of God's Word and His promises.

"You're not cold, you're not hot—far better to be either cold or hot!"

REVELATION 3:15 MSG

91

Applies to You

You may have checked the category "does not apply" on an application or survey form. Even if the question applies to every other respondent, it is not relevant to you or your situation. Most of us, at one time or another, have chosen the "does not apply" option concerning some aspect of life. Perhaps we felt that "Don't walk on the grass" didn't mean us; or the posted speed limit concerned other drivers, but not ourselves (at least when there was no patrol car in sight).

Now when God says to you in the words of scripture that He loves the whole world, do you make yourself an exception? Do you think that Jesus atoned for all sins, minus the ones you have committed? Do you, in the depths of your heart, feel that His Spirit's assurances of joy and peace don't apply to you?

If any one or all of these questions do, in fact, apply to you, you're not alone. Just as the seemingly poised and self-assured speaker at the podium may have butterflies in her stomach the whole time, sincere and honest believers often harbor thoughts of shame and unworthiness. There's always a nagging suspicion that when God whispers, *"I love you,"* He doesn't mean *you*. Conscious of your weaknesses, you mentally check "does not apply."

But it *does* apply to you because your heavenly Father says it does. He promises you, child of God, forgiveness, mercy, compassion, love, and eternal life with Him in heaven. Through His Spirit at work in you, He provides hope and strength, peace of mind and joy of heart. Today, with confidence and thanksgiving, check and receive "all of the above."

Do not throw away this confident trust in the Lord. Remember the great reward it brings you!

HEBREWS 10:35 NLT

Receive His Gifts

When an agency serving the community solicits donations, they start by saying what they need and why they need it. A food pantry, for example, explains that they need nonperishable goods because their shelves are empty. An animal shelter requests towels for kennels or funds to help defray the cost of veterinary services.

Imagine our astonishment when we arrive at the pantry with several cartons of canned meats and vegetables, but they turn us away! Imagine our shock when we hand a check and a stack of towels to the receptionist at the shelter, but it's handed back to us! Wouldn't happen, would it? There are times, however, when we cry out in desperate need and then reject the one who supplies it.

When we experience genuine sorrow for sins and shortcomings, we turn to God, begging His forgiveness, crying out to Him to lift the weight of our guilt and restore our rest and peace of mind. He hears our cry! And His Spirit calls to mind Jesus' death and resurrection, the promise of new life in Him, and His ability and willingness to completely wipe the slate clean. But what happens? We contemplate these truths, realize they are exactly what would meet our needs, and then refuse to apply them to ourselves!

God desires to serve your every spiritual need, including the need for forgiveness. His Son Jesus came into the world for no other reason than to show the extent of His compassion and caring. During His earthly ministry, He healed people who cried out to Him and strengthened people who knew they were weak—people like you. Make your every need known to Him; and when He comes to you, receive the gifts He brings.

God so loved the world that he gave his one and only Son, that whoever believes in him shall not perish but have eternal life.

JOHN 3:16 NIV

No Thank You

Here's good advice to follow if an unwanted sales caller continues to talk after you've said, "No thank you." Hang up! Because if you stay on the line, you're likely to give out more information about yourself than you ever intended. Clever callers will be able to spot a vulnerable point and use it to their advantage.

When you entertain doubts about God's love for you or His presence in your life, you're offering an opening to disbelief. While you may think you can hold your own in a conversation with doubt, little by little, doubt will win. Every reason you bring up for not doubting, doubt will counter with another doubt. Soon your reasons for not doubting God's promises will come to an end, and that's when your wily opponent will "close the sale." You've bought what you never, ever meant to purchase—disbelief!

There's a difference between constructive doubts that you should explore and destructive doubts that prey on you. The former will not shake your trust in God but will motivate you to search the Bible, open commentaries, and talk to others to find a meaningful answer. What have you bought? Increased knowledge and strengthened faith! The latter will prick at your spiritual well-being, lead you in circular arguments, and destroy your peace of mind. Your purchase? Human logic and crumbled faith!

"No thank you," and hang up immediately—there could be no better advice to take when doubts come calling. Turn to God for a rich supply of everything you need: faith, trust, and complete reliance on His Word. Enjoy the comfort of a long and productive conversation with Him.

Don't turn away God's Spirit.

1 THESSALONIANS 5:19 CEV

Terms of Believing

A writer for a local newspaper interviewed a man who said that he would believe in God only if God offers him proof of His existence. "Appear in front of me," the man suggested as acceptable proof. "Work a miracle or something." Although scores of Christians replied to the article with love and compassion, offering testimony about how God had touched their hearts and worked miracles in their lives, the man remained adamant. He demanded proof on *his* terms.

What he failed to understand is this: faith is a gift. But unlike an obliging husband at Christmastime who asks his wife what size to buy, where to buy it, and what color to choose, God already knows. After all, He created us! He knows exactly the faith that will fit our present needs, at what time to supply it, and in what manner His Spirit will give it to us. When God is the giver, the gift is given on the giver's terms, not those of the recipient.

God's terms? They're easy and pleasant. He asks nothing but that you accept faith with a humble heart and receptive mind, believe in His Son Jesus Christ, rely on His promises, and trust His Spirit to nurture and develop your faith according to His will. It's not a onetime gift, either, but an everyday gift, constantly building in strength and vigor as you use it and depend on it. There's a bonus gift too: when you surrender human reason to God-given faith, you begin to find all the proof you need of His power and His presence. It's when you recognize His presence and see miracles happen.

In all circumstances take up the shield of faith, with which you can extinguish all the flaming darts of the evil one.

EPHESIANS 6:16 ESV

Caring Teacher

For students who demonstrate special aptitude for a subject, a good teacher challenges them by creating extra opportunities for them to hone their skills. The whole class isn't expected to advance as quickly or go as high, but the teacher knows what talented and dedicated students can do with the right tools and guidance.

Your good teacher, God, knows what you're capable of. He knows your strong points and your weak points, and how committed you are to learning His Word and His ways. But He will never bark, "You! Do more!" and then leave you to your own devices. No good teacher would do such a thing. Rather, His Spirit, living in you, enables you to advance spiritually. He equips you with the inner tools you need—strength, faith, resolve, endurance, perseverance, wisdom—to resist temptation and overcome challenges.

Like any good teacher, God will not expose you to a temptation beyond your God-given ability to resist. He will use the challenges that He permits to enter your life in any number of ways—to stretch your experience and know-how; to increase your reliance on Him; to show you how capable you really are; to demonstrate to you His power at work in you; to enable you to better understand and help those who may later undergo similar trials.

If your challenges seem particularly difficult today, see your good teacher. Ask Him to give you the spiritual, emotional, and material tools you need to tackle your special "assignment." Rely on Him to empower you with patience, renew you with His presence, and bless you with the encouragement and support of others. You will be surprised at what you can do!

God blesses those who patiently endure testing and temptation.

JAMES 1:12 NLT

Inner Peace

For decades, Clara had happily served her family, church, and community. Her exemplary conduct received the admiration of others, and no one doubted her honesty and integrity. If you needed anything from practical help to spiritual guidance, you could rely on Clara to willingly and gladly take care of you. Outwardly, she was the perfect Christian woman.

But elderly and unable to do as much as she once did, Clara's thoughts turned inward. Long nighttime hours brought to mind the woman in her congregation who, though she did little work, always seemed to garner more recognition than Clara. Her unbelieving friend who, despite frequent invitations, never once visited Clara's church. Her adult son who, rejecting his Christian upbringing, followed an irresponsible lifestyle.

Shame enveloped her like a shroud. Had she served all those years only to win the praise of others? Was the joy of Christ so muted in her life that her best friend never saw the value of faith? What did she do wrong that caused her son to make so many poor life choices? Hot tears seeped from Clara's eyes: she was not, and never had been, a real Christian!

A logical conclusion for Clara, but not for God. When Clara was willing to listen to His voice, she heard that no human effort is completely unsullied by selfish motivation. No Christian—only the Holy Spirit—can convert another. We only invite and encourage. No mother, no matter how capable, can control the life of her children.

The assurance of God's love and forgiveness allowed Clara the peace she craved. Your heavenly Father offers the same to you.

God will bless you with peace that no one can completely understand. And this peace will control the way you think and feel.

PHILIPPIANS 4:7 CEV

Sure Success

"Whether you think you can, or you think you can't," American industrialist Henry Ford once said, "you're right." Perhaps you remember a time when you set out to do something, and despite detours, hindrances, and struggles along the way, you did it. Your success surprised those around you, and it may have surprised you as well. Nonetheless, you knew, deep down inside, that you had what it took to succeed, and your confidence saw you through to the end.

Reality-based confidence makes a difference, most especially in spiritual matters. If you were to lack confidence in God's love for you, it's unlikely you would trust Him to receive you with open arms when you go to Him. You might make a few halfhearted steps in His direction, but the slightest doubts or misgivings would stop you in your tracks. Firm beliefs, however, would dismiss the doubts and help you keep on going to Him. A positive frame of mind can make the difference between divine comfort and human despair, heaven-sent solace and earthly distress.

When it comes to temptation (and temptation comes to everyone!), what you think is crucial. If you think you can't overcome it by yourself, you're absolutely right. Not one of us, by our own resolution or intention, can conquer temptation. But if you think the Holy Spirit dwelling within you can give you the ability to overcome temptation, you're absolutely right again. He can, and He will.

If a particular temptation disturbs you today, think— believe!—that you can resist it with the help of God's Spirit. Remain confident in His power, keep going forward, and never give up because your success is assured.

God has not given us a spirit of fear and timidity, but of power, love, and self-discipline.

2 TIMOTHY 1:7 NLT

Going Places

Two longtime friends, Deb and Carla, were enjoying lunch as they sat on the patio of a local café. During the conversation, Deb began to tease Carla by bringing up the time she fell for a coworker's office prank. "Oh," laughed Carla, "let's not even go there!"

Temptation likes to bring up the past, often when you least expect it, and always adds a suggestion for you. An insult you suffered last year: Shouldn't you feel offended? Shouldn't you get back at him? That sin you committed and asked God to forgive: Wait a minute! Do you believe God *really* has forgotten this? A new trend or fashion: Everyone's doing it. You should try this, at least once, don't you think?

But you say: "Let's not even go there!" With God's power enabling you, swat temptation as you would a pesky mosquito. In doing so, you're keeping yourself from committing the sin and from the remorse sure to follow. You're also allowing the Holy Spirit to strengthen you so you'll become more and more able to withstand other temptations that come your way. And you can rest assured they will for as long as you live this side of heaven!

Joyful in His presence, go where God will lead you and where His love is sure to keep you.

"If you keep my commands,
you'll remain intimately
at home in my love."

JOHN 15:10 MSG

Temptation's Mask

Here's an unlikely newspaper advertisement: "Buy this product and rue the day you did!" An email you'll never see: "Hey! Open this attachment—and by the way, it's a virus!" No, if someone wants to trick you, they need to persuade you that you're getting a bargain if you buy or that you're receiving a document from a trusted source.

Temptation never identifies itself as harmful or dangerous. Instead, it wears the mask of legitimacy and authenticity. It drapes itself in attractiveness and popularity, satisfaction and happiness, modernity and sophistication. With its dancing shoes donned, temptation lures all comers to skip along for good times, laughter, and fun.

You already know what happens. Perhaps you can think of a time when you or someone you love found it convenient or appealing to speak or act against God's commandments. Or now you realize that bit of "harmless" gossip led to a smeared reputation. That occasional indulgence opened the door to full-fledged addiction. That seemingly minor lapse morphed into a severed relationship with others and with God. There are as many examples as there are sins, and each one serves as a warning against giving in to temptation.

If a thought or suggestion, decision or opportunity would take you away from God's commandments, lift its mask. Underneath you will see nothing but the ugly face of temptation staring right back at you. Do not buy; do not click. Obey the one who truly wants the best for you.

Watch out for false prophets!
They dress up like sheep,
but inside they are wolves who
have come to attack you.

MATTHEW 7:15 CEV

No and Yes

Even when, with God's help, you wholeheartedly reject temptation, it comes back. Sometimes it returns in the same form day after day, on each occasion tantalizing you with the identical "reward," and you keep repeating your resounding "No!" It's possible that this sin will entice you for years, decades, or even a lifetime, but your every refusal gradually weakens its pull. Meanwhile, God's Spirit is building solid strength in you, and you're all the better able to stand firm despite temptation's allure.

In other instances, a resisted temptation may leave you and not come back. This happened to Lois, who, as a child, fought the temptation to steal from a neighborhood retailer. Later, as a sales associate in a store, she realized she had not the slightest desire to take anything that wasn't hers. But another temptation, even stronger than the first, took its place. She often waited on wealthy women, many her own age, and they bought whatever struck their fancy. Lois, to make ends meet, had to work until late almost every evening, and she often overheard her customers' plans to play tennis the next morning or go away for the weekend. Envy and resentment, new temptations, hammered at Lois's peace of mind every day.

Though its shape may change as your situation changes, temptation will hover around you, waiting for your yes. Don't hesitate to ask God for His power to say no to all temptations, both old and new, and to keep saying no for as long as you need. Pray without doubting that His answer to you is yes.

Consider it pure joy, my brothers and sisters, whenever you face trials of many kinds, because you know that the testing of your faith produces perseverance.

JAMES 1:2–3 NIV

Better Route

We sincerely promise to help a friend over the weekend, but when Saturday morning arrives, we've forgotten all about it. It's only when we see her the following week that our words come to mind—uh-oh! Embarrassed, we apologize profusely for letting her down, hoping she'll understand.

Remembering the sting of embarrassment, we can react in one of two ways. First, we can decide never to offer our help again to anyone. Second, we can pledge our assistance but put a note on the calendar so we won't forget again. Most of us will opt for the latter, and better, route. We'll continue to share our time and skills with others, but having learned our lesson, we'll make sure we keep our promises.

When we fail to keep a promise we've made to ourselves, however, we have three choices. First, we can tell ourselves that "it's just the way I am," or "it's no big deal," and make believe we have nothing to apologize for. Second, we can give up on ourselves and make no further attempts to improve our situation or advance in anything. Third—and this is the better route—we can get up, dust ourselves off, and begin again, this time taking practical steps to avoid the same pitfall.

Spiritually, take the better route. Thank God for His forgiveness, and believe you have received it. Then ask Him for the courage to promise again, armed with wisdom and insight. When your promises to yourself conform to His plans for you, you will be able to keep them. That's His promise to you!

Commit everything you do to
the LORD. Trust him,
and he will help you.

PSALM 37:5 NLT

113

Road Trip

If you like road trips, you know that getting there is half the fun! On the road is where friendships deepen, adventures happen, and laughter stretches for miles. Wrong turns and scenic sites, historical landmarks and surprise encounters come together in a shared memory of the great road trip taken together.

Spiritually, "half the fun" of arriving at our heavenly home lies in the journey it takes to get there. God's gift of life starts us on the road, where our relationship with Him grows as we learn more about Him and His plan for us. Along the way—if we're looking—we discover miracles, uncover truths, and enjoy the wonders of creation. Even our spiritual detours are part of the story because they teach us what *not* to do, enable us to warn others, and show us God's power to get us going again in the right direction.

As with any good road trip, you're not traveling alone. You're on this journey with all who have gone before you, all who have yet to be born, and all in the world today who believe in the saving work of Jesus Christ. You're on the road with wise guides and humble learners, joyful companions and hurting souls. This is where godliness grows and holiness happens, mile after mile after mile.

Enjoy the remarkable journey you're on—the amazing "road trip" that God has planned for you!

I will rejoice in the LORD;
I will take joy in the God
of my salvation.

HABAKKUK 3:18 ESV

Free and Clear

It sounds too easy, doesn't it? After willfully giving in to sinful impulses, or carelessly stumbling into errant ways, God offers the repentant heart complete and immediate forgiveness! Through the strengthening power of the Holy Spirit working within us, God helps us bear the burden of any earthly consequences our actions may have brought upon us. As for eternal consequences, however, it's as if we had never sinned at all.

Now we might imagine that God's forgiveness frees us from taking obedience seriously, knowing that we need simply say to Him, "I'm sorry," and all is forgotten. Not so! With genuine repentance comes a humble recognition that we are weak, along with a sincere desire to put ourselves under the authority of God's good will. This is difficult because we know that the same sin may lure us again, and we wonder if we can wholeheartedly accept God's commandment against it. Repentance pleads for forgiveness and prays for the strength to endure temptation whenever it strikes.

The most difficult part of all, though, is belief in God's ready willingness to forgive. His purpose in sending Jesus was to pay for the guilt of your sins, which He did. He shed His blood for you—proof of how serious sin is in God's eyes—and rose from death for you—proof of how much He wants you to live renewed, restored, and holy in His sight.

Allow Him to lead your repentant heart to the joyous freedom of complete and immediate forgiveness. Let Him open your soul to believe His words to you.

Your sins have been forgiven
on account of his name.

1 JOHN 2:12 NIV

Growing Up

As children, we didn't grow up in a day, and we don't become spiritually mature in a day, either. When we're first hearing about God, we may continue thinking, speaking, and acting in ways quite unlike a Christian because we don't know any better yet. But then as His Spirit nurtures our faith and His Word teaches us His commandments, we begin to see how certain habits, desires, and personal goals are contrary to His will. Once we realize that these things are not acceptable to Him and harmful to us and our relationship with Him, we strive to eliminate them from our lives.

Generally, all this takes place gradually and in its own season. We stumble and fall along the way, just like a toddler learning to walk. Then, as we find that God can and does give us strength in our weakness, we start gaining confidence in our walk with Him. We correct obvious wrongs. His Spirit nudges us to move away from secret sins and hidden vices; He provides discernment so we can identify potential snares and spiritually dangerous situations before we're entrapped by them.

If we knowingly continue doing anything we have come to realize as sinful, however, we're slowing down our progress. We're deliberately withholding obedience to God's will, and that burden (whether a big or small thing, in our opinion) will keep us from becoming spiritual adults in mind, heart, and soul. It will hinder us from experiencing the fullness of faith in Him.

What might be hampering your spiritual growth today? Ask God to help you release it to Him so you can freely, joyfully, and confidently make progress on His path to spiritual maturity.

Strip down, start running—and never quit! No extra spiritual fat, no parasitic sins.

HEBREWS 12:1 MSG

Good Source

Why do bad things happen to good people? You've no doubt heard the subject discussed and debated by believers and nonbelievers alike. It's not fair when innocent people fall victim to violence, or when little children lie in hospital beds with only weeks to live. From the human point of view, it's plain wrong.

In the Bible, God gives us a glimpse of His point of view. He sees a fallen world where wickedness strives to undermine goodness, and evil desires clash with godly hopes and dreams. From the beginning, He put in place a plan of salvation for all humankind, and He sent His Son to fulfill it in a way that only true God/true Man Jesus Christ could. The fact of Jesus' resurrection demonstrates His victory over death, the ultimate evil. Yet God didn't choose to eliminate evil from the world—not yet. Until He does, bad things will continue to happen to good people.

So what can we do about it? We can shake our fist at God or open our hands to help, comfort, heal, and protect.

We can tremble in fear that something bad might befall us at any moment, or rejoice that we have a God who promises to be with us and uphold us through all that may come our way. We can attempt to protect ourselves with money, status, or power; or we can trust Him to take care of us, no matter what takes place in the future.

Is there something bad in your life right now or a fear you can't overcome? Today, share it with your heavenly Father, the source of all that's good.

Who shall separate us from the love of Christ? Shall tribulation, or distress, or persecution, or famine, or nakedness, or danger, or sword?

ROMANS 8:35 ESV

Blessing in Disguise

Have you ever thanked someone for a gift that you neither liked nor wanted? For the sake of politeness, you may have; then as soon as you could, you hid the gift in the attic or gave it away. Obviously, your words of gratitude came not from your heart, but from obligation.

God, like any giver, desires to hear words of thanks. For His many blessings in your life, you find them easy to say, and they truly come from your heart. But He also invites your thanks for the gifts you don't like, including those you have never asked for and never will. In this case, obligatory phrases won't do because, unlike the well-meaning relative or kindly intentioned friend, God can read your heart.

With sincere gratitude, thank Him, say, for the coworker who drives you crazy. Because of her, you have learned to hold your tongue out of deference for the feelings of another. You know how difficult it is to remain gentle, kind, and patient day after day around people who rub you the wrong way. That's not the norm, you know! But it's your demonstrated strength now, a blessing to your character, and evident advancement in your walk with God.

Again, with genuine appreciation, mention the family member who constantly pushes your buttons. You know that meaningful relationships take effort, compromise, and cooperation. You've had real-life experience, and when a friend shares family-life frustrations, you can offer practical, tried-and-true advice.

If there's someone who constantly gets on your nerves, simply smile and offer a private "thank You" to God for the blessing (and it's probably okay to ask if He might put it in this person's heart to lessen up with the annoying habits too).

Accept each other just as Christ has accepted you so that God will be given glory.

ROMANS 15:7 NLT

Take Me!

"Whatever!" For some parents, their teen's rolled eyes and sigh can drive them to distraction. Yet our heavenly Father has heard the same sigh from many a grown-up believer.

"If I conform my will to God's will," the thinking goes, "then that means I go along with whatever takes place in my life. I don't need to make any effort to make something happen because if it's not His will, I don't want to waste my time with it. If it is His will, it will happen anyway. Whatever!"

Result? A believer bobbing like a buoy on the surface of the sea, carried along on the winds of chance and the tide of current events. Accepting all as "God's will," this believer fails to chart a course, head for a harbor, or even aspire to reach one. Yet a wiser and more perceptive believer could challenge "whatever" with this truth:

Yes, we often surrender our will to God's will. Maturity, experience, and insight can reveal that what we once desired was not worth our life's pursuit. In addition, God has given each of us special talents, gifts, and abilities for a reason, and the reason isn't to squander them by sitting around and waiting for Him to act. No, He intends for us to use all we have to live purposefully and contribute to the world around us. He has blessed us with interests to pursue, goals to reach, and fulfillment to attain, and all that happens not with a resigned sigh of "Whatever!" but with a joyous cry of "Here I am! Take me!"

I am grateful that God always makes it possible for Christ to lead us to victory.

2 CORINTHIANS 2:14 CEV

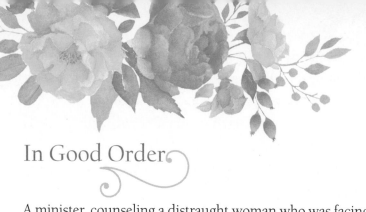

In Good Order

A minister, counseling a distraught woman who was facing a mountain of personal problems, invited her to attend church next Sunday. "Oh, I plan to start going to church again," she assured him, "just as soon as I get my life in order."

Her response could be ours when our troubles pile up, most especially when they're the result of our own poor choices. Before we sit in a pew, we want to put our life in line with God's will. Before we mingle with other churchgoers (who *surely* would not accept us the way we are), we want to appear like one of them. This kind of thinking, however, reveals a misunderstanding of what church really is.

Here's what the minister told the woman: "Church is not a place for perfect people, because they don't need it. Imperfect people do. Come and hear God's words of love for you, and your life will take on new meaning and purpose. Come and receive the comfort and guidance He offers you, and you will have balm for your hurt and strength to change things for the better. Come and look at the people around you—people just like you who long for your acceptance, just as you long for theirs; who need your company, just as you need theirs along the path of life."

When you think "church," what comes to mind? What feelings fill your heart? Do you believe regular church attendance would enrich your life?

Jesus said, "It is not the healthy who need a doctor, but the sick."

MATTHEW 9:12 NIV

Take Your Place

Perhaps you have inherited a cherished family heirloom. It came to you because you were born into a particular family or embraced as one of the family. Whenever you see the heirloom bequeathed to you, you affectionately remember the person who gave it to you and the love he or she felt for you.

That's how God wants you to regard the blessings He has for you. Through faith in His Son Jesus Christ, you have been born into your heavenly Father's family of believers. You have a brother in Jesus, and you're surrounded by countless mothers and fathers and brothers and sisters in Christ. Now the last thing He wants you to do is spend your time and effort working for your place in His family. You already have it. Neither does He want you to turn away the blessings He wants to shower on you, such as joy, peace, and contentment. Take it, and be glad! Take the increased faith He chooses to work in you; the spiritual insights He reveals to you; the knowledge of His love and salvation that He has made known to you. Take it and give thanks because it's yours!

So many of us instinctively turn away from what our Father wants to give us. We think we're not worthy, and this is true. It's not our worthiness that brings us our inheritance, but our place in the family. Or we know we haven't earned it, and this also is true. But again, it's not our earning power that brings us our inheritance, but our place in the family.

What "family heirloom" does God want to give you today? Is it strength, happiness, patience, comfort? Receive it now, and take your place in His family.

If you are Christ's, then you are Abraham's offspring, heirs according to promise.

GALATIANS 3:29 ESV

Blessed Innocence

As we grow older, we become wiser in the ways of the world. We learn by experience and education that we shouldn't trust everyone we meet, believe every statement we hear, or do everything someone might ask us to do. Since we live in an imperfect world, our mental, emotional, and physical well-being depends in large part on our ability to discern between good and bad, constructive and destructive choices.

Earthly practices, however, will only hamper our relationship with God. Because our heavenly Father is loving, holy, and perfect in all His dealings with us, we can dismiss suspicion, caution, and fear. We can wholeheartedly trust Him, completely believe Him, and unhesitatingly obey Him, as a small child would her strong, wise, and loving parent. In our relationship to God, He invites us to become innocent, teachable, tender, and open to the Spirit's work in heart and soul.

We "grow up" in Him when we're willing to become small again. When we're willing to admit our inability to find solid spiritual food, we'll let Him serve us. When we're willing to concede that we can't reach heaven through our own efforts, no matter how high we jump, we'll let Him lift us up. When we're willing to give up thinking we know what's best for us, we'll follow His commandments. We'll become as little children under the care of loving parents.

Today, take note of any areas where you are applying earthly thinking to a heavenly relationship. Ask Him for a spirit of blessed innocence so you can enjoy the full extent of your divine Father's care for you.

Jesus replied, "I tell you the truth, unless you are born again, you cannot see the Kingdom of God."

JOHN 3:3 NLT

Amazing Grace

You're probably familiar with the hymn "Amazing Grace." It's sung in churches, played at commemorative gatherings, and named by many as their favorite spiritual song. Ask someone to define grace, however, and you're likely to get a vague answer, perhaps along the lines of "Well, it's something pretty amazing."

Yes, indeed it is! God's grace, simply stated, is His marvelous love and compassion poured out on undeserving people. His grace moved Him to make Himself known to us in the wonders of creation, the words of scripture, and the whisperings of the human heart. His grace induced Him to provide a way of salvation for a fallen world and to promise full forgiveness for every repentant soul. Today His grace compels Him to extend love even to those who do not love Him and to keep the door wide open for all who return to Him.

God's grace touches your life in both visible and invisible ways. God's grace is working on the outside when He uses your hands to help and comfort; it's working on the inside when you feel content and satisfied with what you have. It can be seen in the example you set and the way you treat others. It can be known in the peace you experience when you embrace His forgiveness.

"Amazing Grace" was written by a sinner in response to God's forgiveness and the gift of faith. How are you responding to His amazing grace toward you?

As God's co-workers we urge you not to receive God's grace in vain.

2 CORINTHIANS 6:1 NIV

Seed of Faith

Faith in the heart is often compared to a garden, and God to a gardener. Here's why: God, because of His grace to you, plants the seed of faith in your heart, and He tends it with perfect love and flawless expertise. In the beginning, faith grows roots and sends up tender green shoots. As it develops, faith blooms with acts of kindness, generosity, and joy. In the winter of struggles, doubt, or difficulties, faith grows deeper and hardier in the hidden places of the heart.

Just as any gardener expects her garden to bloom, God expects your faith in His continuing grace to produce proof of its presence in your life. While in some seasons, you will find it easy and joyous to follow Him; in others, you may find it difficult to go on. Now you have a choice because you can allow His Spirit to nurture your faith, or you can reject His work and let faith wither for lack of care.

God, the good gardener, desires to keep your faith alive throughout every season of your life. He wants and expects to see your life ablaze with the unique blossoms of your gifts and talents. He promises to keep your faith alive through hardship; to make it tougher and stronger; to make it bloom all the more abundantly at the right time. He does it for love of gardening—for love of you.

Today, thank Him for His grace to you and how your faith in Him has grown. Let Him fill your heart with the hope and promise of abundance in seasons yet to come.

I am the true vine, and my Father is the gardener.

JOHN 15:1 CEV

Can't Help It

A blade of grass peeks through a tiny crack in the concrete. Wildflowers dot a hillside ravaged by forest fire. Stems emerge under a layer of melting snow. Against all odds, fertile seeds will grow—it's what God created them to do, and they do it, even under tough conditions.

God makes faith grow too. When He plants the seed of faith in our hearts, faith will grow without any anxiety on our part. He tends our faith and nourishes it as we read and meditate on His words to us. This simply happens because that's the way He created faith. We don't have to wonder whether our faith is growing, because it is. He strengthens our faith as we rely on Him to help us meet the challenges we face and apply His promises to our real-life circumstances. There's never a need to doubt that faith will carry us through, because it will. Faith, willingly received, just can't help but do what God has created it to do.

In hardship, hold on to faith, because it will find a way to grow. In a heart seared by grief, trust faith to find a place of comfort and rest. In seasons when it seems as if God is silent, believe that faith still thrives and vibrant life will bloom again.

Do you not know that you are God's temple and that God's Spirit dwells in you?

1 CORINTHIANS 3:16 ESV

Values Applied

Jane and Joseph, parents of two teen boys, frequently visited Jane's widowed mother. Although Grandma had been doing well living on her own, the couple started to see unsettling signs of change. After discussing the matter, the couple invited Grandma into their home. Grandma did not welcome the suggestion, but after several health scares, she relented. Jane thanked God. "She cared for me when I was young," Jane said, "and now God has given me a chance to give back to her."

But after months of accommodating her mom's doctor's appointments, special diet, and adamant demands, Jane was exhausted. Joseph and the boys resented the way Grandma changed their home, and Jane felt torn between devotion to her mother and loyalty to her family. More than she would admit to herself, she no longer wanted the God-given task she had taken on so happily.

Jane's dilemma is not unusual. We bring a certain energy and optimism to new tasks that rarely carry us through to the end, and a time of testing arrives. A time of sorting through principles we're prepared to apply to our real-life circumstances. A time of asking for God's strength, help, and wisdom to guide us as we meet each day.

If you were Jane, what would you do? Your answer reflects the values you believe are most important. Are they God's values? If so, how have you applied these values to your life circumstances?

Put everything to the test.
Accept what is good.

1 THESSALONIANS 5:21 CEV

Blissful Living

"Do what you love" and "follow your bliss" are only two of numerous slogans urging you to do whatever you believe will bring you happiness. Proponents promise you that, free from responsibilities to others, you will find fulfillment for yourself.

Suppose you took their advice. Now your preferences alone determine your decisions. Your opinion alone decides what you will do, where you will go, and with whom. But your fantasy of short-term fun ends when you consider the long-term consequences, most notably severed relationships with supportive friends and relatives—and with God. Whenever self's desires come before God's desires, true freedom, genuine fulfillment, and lasting joy are no longer possible.

We are changeable, and what satisfies one day won't the next. We are shortsighted, and what might seem okay now may not stand the test of time. We are often mistaken, and we look for happiness in all the wrong places. Our unchangeable, all-knowing, and holy God desires our eternal good. Our full acceptance of His will gives us the ability to find joy in our circumstances, the wisdom to know what needs to be changed and what needs to stay the same, and the power to make a positive difference in our lives and in the lives of those around us. His will is where our fulfillment, purpose, and meaning reside. He is our true source of bliss!

In all things, let His will become your will. That way, no matter what you are doing, you will be doing what you love.

The world and all its wanting, wanting, wanting is on the way out—but whoever does what God wants is set for eternity.

1 JOHN 2:17 MSG

Successful Living

Thomas did not look like a football player. A tall, lanky, skinny kid, he seemed more suited to track or basketball. But being on the football team was his goal, and he pursued it. He spent untold hours working out, building strength, learning plays, and bearing the taunts of huskier boys. When tryouts came, you guessed it—Thomas made the team.

But what if he had not succeeded, despite his best efforts? He would have been disappointed, of course. Until he grew older, however, he would not understand that he, in fact, had succeeded at things far more important and longer lasting than being on the team. He learned how to pinpoint a destination and plan practical steps to get there. How to remain focused on the goal, even when days are long, practice is monotonous, and progress is slow. How to ignore disparaging remarks from those who delight in tearing others down. How to take pride in productive work done well, even when the outcome is not assured.

By following God's plan for your life, you're not guaranteed earthly success, either. You may or may not hear "thanks" from the lips of someone you helped in a big way, receive admiration for enduring a difficult situation, or gain public recognition for standing up for justice. Of this you're certain, however: you'll experience the power of God's Spirit making a difference in your life. You'll possess peace of mind for having done the right and honorable thing. You'll get to sleep soundly with the comfort of a clear conscience. You'll know, enabled by His Spirit within you and despite obstacles and stumbles along the way, you gave your best effort.

What is success for you? How does earthly success compare to heavenly success? Can you have both?

I've got my eye on the goal, where God is beckoning us onward—to Jesus. I'm off and running, and I'm not turning back.

PHILIPPIANS 3:14 MSG

Easy Living

God never expects us to do for others what He doesn't first do for us. His forgiveness teaches us to forgive others; His love enables us to love others; and His example, through the person of Jesus Christ, shows us how to help, heal, and encourage others in practical and meaningful ways.

Through the presence of His Spirit in us, God continues His life-changing work in us so we can do the same for others. He equips us to gladly take on difficult roles—such as parent, teacher, caregiver, and the like—by allowing us to see Him in the faces of those who need our help. He motivates us to give generously of our time, abilities, and resources to others by replenishing us with treasures that will last for eternity. He encourages us to patiently persevere in our God-given tasks by endowing us with the rewards of earned self-esteem, productive goals, and inner peace.

Just as others may look to you for help, you can look to God for all the assistance you need on your spiritual journey. If it's motivation to begin a difficult task, ask His

Spirit to grant you enthusiasm and renew your frame of mind. Support to keep going? Ask Him to send someone to share the load. Joy for the road? Ask Him to open your eyes to His presence and the love He has for you!

"My yoke is easy and
my burden is light."

MATTHEW 11:30 NIV

Best Manager

One of the responsibilities of a corporate manager is to put the right people in the right jobs. Good managers spend time talking with prospective employees, discovering their interests and goals, and assessing their strengths and weaknesses. After they hire people, these managers see that they get everything they need to perform their work efficiently and successfully.

You know that God is the best of managers, and He never makes a hiring mistake. When you turn to Him and ask Him what He would have you do, rest assured you will be put in the right position at the right time. Rely on Him to equip you for the work He gives you because He will. He's that kind of manager.

Now in the workplace, the manager notices someone she believes has the potential to handle increased responsibilities and take on weightier tasks. She'll talk to the employee and outline the plans she has in mind. Though the employee may feel completely unqualified, he trusts his manager's judgment.

Knowing he'll receive ongoing support and thankful for the vote of confidence, he eagerly accepts the opportunity to advance.

God does that too. If a God-given opportunity opens in front of you, why hesitate to take it? If God thinks you're the right person for the job, you are—trust Him. If you lack guidance, skill, or know-how, He'll provide a way for you to acquire it. And be thankful because God has chosen you.

"My grace is all you need.
My power works best in weakness."

2 CORINTHIANS 12:9 NLT

Serve-Ability

Do you know the fastest route to burnout? Attempt to do everything yourself! Make it your task today to vacuum the carpet, repair the roof, cook for the kids, wash their clothes, and attend their soccer game. Put it on your planner to write a twenty-page report, facilitate a meeting, choose office furniture, answer your emails, and settle an employee dispute. Volunteer to sing in the choir, teach Sunday school, visit the sick, take books to the shut-ins, and serve meals at the homeless shelter. Whew! Makes you tired just to think about it, doesn't it?

No matter where you are in life, God has something for you to do. Maybe even several "somethings," but never everything. While you may find yourself willing and able to serve in multiple God-pleasing ways, you are limited by the number of hours in a day, your need for rest and recreation, and the demands of your God-given obligations and responsibilities. Push the boundaries, and you're inviting stress and frustration into your life.

In all likelihood, you have the ability to do many things well, but don't try to do them all. You may be in a position to teach, equip, and encourage others to share in the joy of serving, and you can delegate some tasks. Or you can focus on a specific expertise, talent, and interest by advancing your knowledge and effectiveness in that field. Or you might pursue one path in particular because your unique circumstances at the moment make you the obvious person to step forward. Right now, there's a special way you can be God's hands in His world—but remember, He has given you only two hands!

Do your best to win God's approval as a worker who doesn't need to be ashamed and who teaches only the true message.

2 TIMOTHY 2:15 CEV

Moving Forward

Many volunteers who accept a leadership role in a club or on a committee have found that once they're in, it's hard to get out! No one comes forward to take their place, and so they stay on year after year when they would prefer to move on to something else.

As in secular life, we can get stuck in our spiritual life too. Whether we serve within a congregation or religious fellowship, or embrace a role we feel God has called us to, we can reach a point of stagnation. We find ourselves doing the same thing year after year, well beyond the time we realize that we would like to try something new, or new circumstances have opened new opportunities. But we're typecast by others—or we have typecast ourselves—and we don't know how to change.

Simply put, you change by making a change. Announce you will serve your term but will not be available for reelection, and stick to it. Offer help and training to anyone interested in following you, and trust that the Lord will send someone, just as He sent you. Then, when your term is up, step into the new role you have chosen. The same holds true to less structured roles you may occupy. Leave with grace, thankful for the opportunity to have contributed, friendships made, and lessons learned; and go forward with grace, glad for the personal growth, spiritual development, and new experiences ahead of you.

The old joke about rejecting change "because we've always done it that way" holds true with personal identity too. If God is calling you to move ahead, trust Him to take care of whatever He is calling you to leave behind.

I heard the voice of the Lord saying, "Whom shall I send? And who will go for us?" And I said, "Here am I. Send me!"

Isaiah 6:8 NIV

151

Untroubled Past

In almost any situation we have come through, we can look back and see things we did well and things we could have done better. For an objective assessment of strengths and weaknesses, hindsight is a useful tool. But more often than not, we blur twenty-twenty hindsight with personal emotions and subjective opinion.

Say we like to put ourselves in a good light. In that case, we describe our right actions in glowing terms and cover our mistakes with self-serving excuses. If we're self-critical, however, we shine a beam on things we wish we hadn't done, and we mentally beat ourselves up over each one. What we did right lingers in the shadows, dismissed as unimportant.

God's guidelines give us a more accurate picture. Look back, humbly noting your instances of obedience to God's will and your successes at accomplishing what you had set out to do. Give thanks to Him! And then confess where you fell short of your expectations and His, sincerely asking for His forgiveness and for better actions next time. Give thanks to Him!

If hindsight fills you with excessive pride or weighs you down with regret, pray that God will show you how to look at the past. There's no better way to light today and tomorrow.

Let God transform you into a new person by changing the way you think.

ROMANS 12:2 NLT

Belief in Action

In prayer, we tell God what we hope He will do for us. We hope He will receive our love, forgive our sins, supply our needs, and accept our thanks for His goodness to us. But it's our after-prayer actions that show what we actually believe God will do for us.

If we do not simply hope God loves us but believe the reality of it, how could we feel anything but joyful? If we believe He sent His Son to take the punishment for our sins, how could we entertain any doubts of our worth in His eyes or our place in His heart? If we believe Jesus rose from the tomb in victory, how could we wonder whether God has completely forgiven the sin we just confessed?

We pray for our daily bread—all the physical needs of our body and the material needs and desires for day-to-day life—yet worry incessantly about having enough and work frantically to get more. We pray for spiritual needs like kindness, compassion, faithfulness, and love but forget to put them into practice. Do we believe He has given them to us? We gratefully list our blessings and humbly accept our hardships; but if we're thankful for what we have and believe in His good judgment, why does discontent disturb our thoughts?

When you pray, don't merely hope God will come through for you. Show Him with your actions that you actually believe He will meet your every need according to His good will.

When you ask, you must believe and not doubt, because the one who doubts is like a wave of the sea, blown and tossed by the wind.

JAMES 1:6 NIV

Real Rest

A nap during the day refreshes body and mind, but when God offers rest, He speaks of an even more essential kind of relaxation. He invites us to receive soul-deep rest, the kind designed to last no matter how hard we work or how many hours of activity we cram into our days.

Our heavenly Father knows how constant anxiety drains energy and shadows our emotions. We can't enjoy what we're doing if we're worried it won't turn out right, no matter how much time and effort we put into it. We'll never know true joy if we're gripped by continual discontent, anger, envy, or bitterness. We're unable to take pleasure in our God-given responsibilities if we think that another person's role is more appealing, attractive, attention getting, and easier than our own. We won't grow spiritually if nagging guilt over past sins churns within us in a perpetual cycle of shame and regret.

Your heavenly Fathers knows you. That's why He begs you to accept the rest that will change your life. Give your anxieties to Him and receive Spirit-enabled trust in His wisdom, control, and authority over all aspects of your life. Ah! What freedom! Let go of discontent and take in Spirit-empowered thanks for the responsibilities He has entrusted to you and challenges He will see you through. Ah! What strength! Confess the regrets that so depress you and believe that He fully forgives and completely restores the repentant soul. Ah! What peace!

If you can, take a nap. You'll feel better all day. But if you want to feel good for a lifetime, take His kind of rest.

Take the yoke I give you. Put it on your shoulders and learn from me. I am gentle and humble, and you will find rest.

MATTHEW 11:29 CEV

Signs of God

God has provided us with many signs of His existence. He created the universe with its wonders and mysteries to draw our thoughts outward and upward. He designed oceans, seas, flowers, grasses, and trees that draw us to seek the master artist; and He gave life to fish, birds, and myriad animals so we could mirror His compassion toward all living things.

God breathed life into us, his highly complex creatures capable of communication, thought, reflection, and action. He gave us the ability to comprehend and create; innovate and invent; and experience emotions like love and joy, pleasure and satisfaction. Within us He put a conscience so we can clarify right from wrong, and He set a soul with a longing for Him as natural as the stomach's yearning for food. And then, so no one could miss Him, He revealed Himself in the words of scripture so all could follow Him in confidence and certainty.

But in this fallen world, many refuse to find in the universe anything more than a mixture of gasses, and see no more in creation than scenic vistas, delightful beaches, and splendid sunsets. They discern nothing in the human body other than chemicals and reproducing cells and no particular God-likeness in the ability to think, create, plan, and do. And their own innate hunger for meaning and purpose? They feed it with schemes and ideas of their own making. Their questions of life's beginning and its end? Those can be ignored when you're between the two.

Many people you meet today may be among those who will never find God in scripture, either, because they'll never read it. The only sign of God they'll ever see on earth is you.

Your very lives are a letter that anyone can read by just looking at you. Christ himself wrote it—not with ink, but with God's living Spirit.

2 CORINTHIANS 3:2–3 MSG

The Answer

Perhaps one of the most difficult teachings of scripture for today's Christians is Jesus' claim that faith in Him is the sole path to God. It's a difficult statement for many to accept when other religions present their own paths to spiritual fulfillment. And then some will say that sincerity of belief, not the belief itself, leads to spiritual fulfillment. Unless we're extremely persuasive orators and well versed in world religions, we'll never be able to hold our own in a debate on the matter! Yet we're given an even more powerful way to make our case: live as Jesus lived.

The reality of a transformed life is impossible to argue against, and it's clear for all to see. In an age of rampant materialism, someone who isn't grasping for money and status stands out. When dire headlines cause many to despair, someone who remains confident and levelheaded is noticed. Where cynicism and skepticism keep all beliefs at arm's length, someone whose warm smile and welcoming eyes reflect a God-centered soul is remembered. Who doesn't respond to helpful gestures, kind expressions, encouraging words, courageous acts, generous giving, genuine forgiveness, simple trust, and unselfish love? And it's then they may ask how you keep such a positive attitude, handle your hardships with such grace, maintain serenity in a chaotic world.

Your life has already stated your position, so there's no debate, just a question: What makes your life different? What are you so confident about? All you need to do is give them a simple and truthful answer. What is it?

---

*"You are the light of the world.
A city set on a hill cannot be hidden."*

MATTHEW 5:14 ESV

161

Go Ahead!

"Something just told me to go over and say hi to her," a woman told the paramedic, "and I'm so glad I did." As the ambulance sped away, she recounted to bystanders how she had seen the young girl sitting alone at a bus stop. As the woman approached the bench, she saw her clutching her swollen abdomen, her face taut with terror. "Honey. . . ," she gasped as she pulled out her cell phone and called 911. Later, she learned that it was her intervention that had saved the girl's prematurely born baby.

Not all God's promptings involve life-and-death situations, but each reveals His work in the world. Though all Spirit-inspired acts of kindness and generosity result in a happy ending, you may never hear of it—like how your warm greeting touched the heart of an older woman who was feeling unnoticed and unloved; how your good humor in the long line at the airport calmed another passenger's frayed nerves; how the sound of your laughter brought a smile to the lips of a middle-aged man who hadn't laughed in a long, long time.

With so much giving, what do you get in return? To know, all you need to do is put yourself in the place of the woman whose concern for a stranger saved a life. Imagine feeling invisible to the world, and then suddenly someone treats you as if you're somebody, even somebody special. Imagine being the person who made you feel that way! If you knew what a difference your lighthearted comment made to the stressed-out passenger in front of you, you would congratulate yourself. If you were aware how delightful your laughter is to the ears of others, you would—well, laugh all the more. So go ahead!

Be glad in God!

PHILIPPIANS 3:1 MSG

163

Heroic Love

From childhood on, we stand in awe of heroes! Once we watched wide eyed as cartoon heroes scaled skyscrapers and pictured ourselves accomplishing the same feat. Now we honor real-life heroes who serve their country at great personal risk. We hesitate to step into their shoes, however, wondering if we would prove equally as brave in similar circumstances.

In our walk with God, we hear of believers today who heroically hold to their faith despite ridicule, fines, job loss, imprisonment, or worse. How many of us would remain so faithful? Thanks to God's mercy, most of us will never undergo that test. Yet we are required to be faithful. Our challenge is to forgive not just our friends but our enemies; love not just people who love us in return but people who disappoint us, or even despise us. God calls us to obedience, even when personal desire pulls us the other way; to generosity toward others, even when our own resources are dwindling; to patience, even when we're short tempered after a long and tiring day.

God invites you to pray for those who suffer for their faith because the same Spirit that gives them the power to stand firm also infuses you with the power to consistently show His love to those around you in practical, everyday ways. Though less noted in the eyes of the world, your Spirit-enabled words and actions are just as important in the eyes of God.

Few of us are called to perform heroic actions, but all of us are called to do ordinary things with heroic love.

We truly love God only when we obey him as we should, and then we know that we belong to him.

1 JOHN 2:5 CEV

Faith-Building Exercise

If you have ever joined a gym, it's likely that a trainer introduced you to the equipment you were free to use. Unless you already had body-building experience, the trainer would advise you to start slow at first. Don't lift the heaviest weights until you can lift lighter ones! Don't expect to run three laps around the track if running one lap leaves you gasping for air! You'll only injure yourself and perhaps turn away from the exercise program altogether.

Faith building goes the same way. God won't ask you to overcome something that you don't have sufficient Spirit-given power to overcome. If He sends a challenge your way, trust Him that you can meet it. You either have the strength within you now, or He will provide it in some fashion as you go along. Whether you anticipate a fairly quick resolution or lengthy process, God will enable you to get through it. The important part for you is your willingness to accept whatever task He puts in front of you. If it's from the hand of God, you're spiritually strong enough to take it on.

When you're faced with tough times, take comfort in remembering that you are not following someone who has never experienced temptation, abuse, grief, and loss. Jesus walked this earth to show you He knows and cares, and most comforting of all, He's been there. Pray, because He understands what you're talking about. Walk with Him, because He's traveled the path before and He knows the way out.

My God has become my strength.

Isaiah 49:5 ESV

Time Tested

Interest may draw you to another person, but lasting friendships, as well as romantic love, mature slowly. Bonds between people strengthen less from one spectacular show of affection than from countless small, thoughtful gestures. More than from a single grand expression of love, we respond to ordinary, heartfelt, and consistent actions showing that the person cares about us. Only after time has tested our attraction are we likely to commit the heart.

Your Spirit-inspired interest in spiritual life requires no instant commitment, either. Certainly, something dramatic could happen, like a miraculous healing or unexplainable rescue, but that's not the norm; and it wouldn't necessarily result in lasting faith anyway. Rather, God leads you to love Him by gradually and quietly opening Himself to you, awakening the eyes of your soul to His power and His presence. He stirs you to do something seemingly inconsequential—help a stranger, comfort a child, take time for a loved one—and you do it and receive His warm, gentle peace in your soul. After time has proven to you that God's love for you is true, and you have proven to yourself that you want to follow His whisperings in your heart, then the time of commitment has come.

Where are you in your relationship with God? If it is just beginning, let each day reveal more of His way with you. Let yourself respond to His promptings. Let your faith take root. If time has proven the goodness of His love, commit your heart to Him. He will never fail you.

Open your mouth and taste, open your eyes and see—how good GOD is.

PSALM 34:8 MSG

Gift of Giving

Suppose someone you love showers you with everything your heart desires but refuses to accept anything from you. Though you thoughtfully pick out gifts you believe would be appreciated and painstakingly create beautiful handmade articles, this person receives none of it. Soon your delight in receiving fades because you yearn to give back but can't.

Healthy, mature love between two people includes the ability and willingness to give as well as take. Though each member of the couple brings different gifts to the relationship, each receives with gratitude and shares with pleasure. This is the way a joyful, wholesome relationship with God goes too. Although He is complete in Himself and the source of your every blessing, He graciously receives your gifts of worship and praise, prayer and thanksgiving. He takes it as your gift to Him when you use your time, abilities, and resources to help the people He loves (and He loves all people). He grants you the privilege of giving not for His sake, but for yours.

If your God-given responsibilities seem burdensome right now, see them as God intends—gifts you can return to Him. They're your way of giving back in a small way for all you have received from Him. Each says "thank You" not in easy words but in selfless endeavor; each declares "I love You" not in a hollow phrase but in observable action. Whatever you have to give Him is ultimately His gift to you—the privilege of sharing and showering His love on others; the privilege of enjoying a mature, healthy relationship with Him.

"Freely you have received;
freely give."

Matthew 10:8 niv

God's Delight

One morning, everything goes wrong. The clothes you had planned to put on are in the wash; you forget to slide the carafe into the coffeemaker, and now there's a mess to clean up; your car won't start. You have every reason to feel more than a little grumpy! What's more, you meet grumpy people all day long—or so it seems. Take another morning when you wake up feeling on top of the world. Everything goes right, and everyone you meet wears a smile—or so it seems.

Our perception of the world around us stems in large part from what we expect to see. That's why God tells us about Himself in His revealed Word. Left on our own, our feelings of fear, guilt, or powerlessness would have us trembling at the thought of a divine judge ready to punish. Scripture tells us that He is full of compassion and eager to forgive. Our experience with life's changes would convince us that we live in an unfeeling universe, but scripture says that God cares about each of us personally. Not just cares, but guides us, comforts us, even delights in us.

Think of someone you take delight in—a child or grandchild, perhaps, whose bubbly, carefree presence brings nothing but joy and laughter. Maybe a beloved pet whose playful antics make you smile every time. That's just a glimpse of the delight God takes in your love and in you.

"He will take delight in you with gladness."

ZEPHANIAH 3:17 NLT

173

Losses and Gains

All too often, we look back on the past and long for what used to be. In those days, we recall, we were young, energetic, beautiful, in love. We had children who needed us and bosses who valued our work. Popular songs reflected our feelings and experiences, and we had no trouble figuring out how to use things. We even earned a few awards and gained a measure of recognition along the way. "Those were the glory days!" we sigh. "And now?"

Now real and lasting glory has a chance to glow in our lives. With every new season of life, we lose the one behind it; yet with every loss, there is gain. As we move past childhood, we gain ability and competence. Leaving young adulthood, we gain experience and maturity. In later years, we gain insight, self-knowledge, and wisdom, plus more time to give to others. As our need to fill a role in the world loses importance, we gain a chance to become more joyfully and genuinely ourselves.

What part of the past still clings to your thoughts?

Gently and mindfully release it into the air as you would a leaf to the wind. Now you have room for God's glory to shine even brighter in your life. Where do you see His light most clearly? What do you have to gain?

There's an opportune time to do things, a right time for everything on the earth.

ECCLESIASTES 3:1 MSG

Beautiful Love

When a couple celebrates their golden anniversary, they're often asked the secret to an enduring marriage. They're likely to mention things like mutual respect, willingness to compromise, perseverance through difficult times, and trust in each other. But suppose they said, "Oh, we *felt* so in love with each other every single day!" You would have reason to question the accuracy of their memories!

No matter how deep your love for God, you will not always experience the sublime beauty of loving feelings. Your emotions, shaded daily by your mood, attitude, and circumstances, do not always tell the truth. One day you might feel abandoned by Him, but the truth? He is always present. Another day you become acutely aware of your shortcomings and feel discouraged in your spiritual progress. The truth? God's arms are open to receive you, forgive you, renew you, and strengthen you. Another day, trouble comes, and feelings whisper that all is lost, but that's not the truth at all. He has found you, redeemed you, and promises you the blessing of life now and forever with Him.

The foundation of an enduring marriage is more than simply happy, loving feelings; it's a commitment to love each other throughout life's changes. This kind of love rejoices and celebrates in good times and supports, encourages, and endures through challenging times. At all times, you can depend on it, and that's the secret of it.

What are your feelings telling you about God? If they differ in any way from how God feels about you, draw close to Him in thought and mind. Let His words lighten your heart and sweeten your thoughts. Rejoice in the "secret" of His love for you.

Three things will last forever—faith, hope, and love—and the greatest of these is love.

1 CORINTHIANS 13:13 NLT

Working Faith

Sandra considered herself a good Christian. She faithfully attended church and Bible class, and she prayed every day. She knew God's commandments and genuinely wanted to obey them, yet real life kept getting in the way. For instance, she didn't feel good when she gossiped about her coworkers, but she told herself that unless she dished out a little, she'd never hear what was really going on in the office. While she didn't use curse words herself, she'd smile lamely when others did because she didn't want them to think her a prude. At the same time, she wondered why no one ever asked her about her faith. Truth is, no one saw it.

"Walk the talk" is essential to our relationship with our Lord in three important ways. First, our words and actions reflect our thoughts and values. For the heart and mind committed to Jesus' teachings, observable behavior flows by necessity and desire. Second, the Lord asks us to put His will ahead of our own. This applies not only to momentous decisions we might face but also to the countless little choices we make every day. Third, He commands us to be His witnesses, and the most powerful and indisputable witness of all is example.

Perhaps there are behaviors or habits in your life where your example doesn't match your Spirit-inspired beliefs and values. Even though you may feel sincere about your faith, visible actions validate it. In addition, the presence of willful faults hinders your spiritual progress and weakens your witness to others. Ask God to help you accept His Word and His will so you can "walk the talk" with increasing boldness and confidence.

Anyone who doesn't breathe is dead, and faith that doesn't do anything is just as dead!

JAMES 2:26 CEV

Soul Mates

What a blessing to know someone you consider your soul mate! With this person you enjoy a rare and precious closeness expressed in your shared dreams and goals; values and principles; perception, attitude, and sense of humor. Though you may not look anything alike, you both feel as if, on some level, you are one and the same.

As God's Spirit continues to shape your thoughts and desires, and as your life gradually conforms to His will, the more you are like His soul mate. As you surrender your desires in favor of His and follow His way instead of your own, you increasingly realize how full, rich, and joyous your relationship feels. You experience His presence because you have it. You act as if you belong to Him because you do.

Ironically, the more of yourself you freely and willingly give to others, the more you become genuinely yourself. Freed from all kinds of spiritual fears and worries, you can enjoy the experience of being alive and take pleasure in the delights of creation. Because of His life in you, you can grieve without hopelessness and mourn without despair. You can smile, laugh, sing, dance, and love with genuine joy.

Prayerfully approach Jesus as your true soul mate. Offer thanks and praise for all the ways He has made you like Him. And then ask Him to show you how your attitude, actions, thoughts, and dreams can even more clearly reflect your divine soul mate.

"If you try to hang on to your life, you will lose it. But if you give up your life for my sake, you will save it."

MATTHEW 16:25 NLT

Look and See

We're all familiar with the old joke about the woman searching frantically for her glasses only to realize she's wearing them. We can laugh because we all have our moments of confusion. But the subject is both serious and sad if we're among the many engaged in a painful struggle to find God. It's serious because God is not hidden at all. It's sad because we can spend years if not a lifetime looking for Him where He does not promise He will be found.

Though our creator has known us from the beginning of time, we fail to know Him as He desires to be known when we look for Him in nature, personal feelings, ideas of what He's like, and human-centered reasoning. Though we may glimpse Him in any or all of these things, we won't be able to fully enjoy His presence unless we look where He is. In scripture, He tells about Himself, His attitude toward us, and His plan of salvation. Fully immersed in scripture, we discover Him in ourselves, where His Spirit dwells, lives, moves, and works in our daily lives.

Once you find Him, you have no need to search any further. Bask in the light of His love, enrich your faith with His wisdom and guidance, and relax in His freely given peace. And laugh because what you have been searching for has been right there all along!

He isn't far from any of us,
and he gives us the power to live,
to move, and to be who we are.

ACTS 17:27–28 CEV

Right to Be Heard

Three generations circled the festive table. The eldest, Grandmother Ella, had invited her children, along with their families, to gather at her home for a sumptuous, home-cooked holiday meal. Before they ate, however, Ella asked for everyone's attention. Only a few heads turned her way. One of her sons rose from his chair, his voice booming. "Show respect for your grandmother!" he demanded. "Your grandmother has a right to be heard!" Now Ella spoke to a quiet room, and everyone heard her voice. But some immediately forgot what she said, so involved were they in their own thoughts; some didn't care, considering her message outdated and irrelevant; only a few listened, cared, and remembered.

Even more than the highest authority or the eldest among us, God has a right to be heard. He is our creator, and He is the source of our blessings each day. Despite the many ways He speaks to us—the words of the Bible, the splendors of creation, the sublimity of music, the guidance of reading, the love of other people—many of us are too busy doing other things to listen. Sometimes He shouts through events and calamities that demand our attention. Caught by surprise, we lift frightened hearts and wringing hands in prayer, scanning the skies for answers. Everyone has heard! But over time, some forget, some stop caring, and only a few still listen, care, and remember.

Of all the voices in your life, make room for God's. Give Him your undivided attention, and do more than simply hear—listen. He has a right to be heard, and you have the privilege of belonging to His family and listening to Him.

"Be still, and know that I am God."

PSALM 46:10 ESV

185

Reasons for Happiness

Someone once said that Christians are the only ones with a reason to be happy. Thanks to God's abundant grace, we know we are loved and cared for, guarded, and guided. We enjoy His strength, forgiveness, peace, and comfort now and the promise of heaven in the future. Why aren't all of us the most positive, upbeat, and optimistic people in the world?

All too frequently, we are focusing on ourselves. We let negative thoughts, volatile emotions, unfortunate circumstances, and other people's shortcomings steal happiness from us. But when we focus on the compassion of our heavenly Father, the presence of His Son, and the gifts of the Holy Spirit, happiness is ours. When we're more interested in lightening the load of others instead of moaning under our own, happiness is ours. When we slam the door on our daily happiness thieves and open ourselves to the joy of living in His love, happiness is ours.

Your genuine happiness could be the most convincing Christian witness you might offer to those who are searching for lasting peace and spiritual joy. God invites you to be happy and live happily, and He showers you with reason after reason to be glad. If you agree, wear happiness in your walk, your talk, your actions—and most of all, on your face.

"Look at me. I stand at the door.
I knock. If you hear me call and
open the door, I'll come right in
and sit down to supper with you."

REVELATION 3:20 MSG

Good Guilt

No one enjoys having a guilty conscience! A guilty conscience accuses, and we don't like being accused. It wakes us in the middle of the night, reminding us of what we have done. It nags us during the day, stinging us with the memory of our wrongdoing. But the most spiritually destructive thing we can do is tell our conscience to be quiet, to go away, to quit bothering us. Because it will. After a time, its voice diminishes and whatever we choose to do feels okay. "Free at last!" we declare, and so we continue in disobedience.

In avoiding the discomfort of a guilty conscience, however, we're throwing aside a valuable spiritual gift. When we go against God's law and ignore His guidance, a Spirit-infused conscience speaks loud and clear: *Come back! Not this way! Stop!* That's a conscience doing its job. Whether human eyes have witnessed our ill-advised actions is of little account when our conscience declares that God's eyes have seen. His voice calls us to repentance, begs us to turn around, fully confess what we have done, and receive

His abundant forgiveness. In believing He has granted it, we discover Spirit-given courage within us to make amends wherever needed. He enables us to strengthen our resolve to avoid temptation in the future. Our conscience at rest, we are truly free.

God corrects you because of love. Allow His Spirit to calibrate your conscience so it will keep you in His path and guide you back if you stray. If there is something your conscience wants to say, listen carefully. Open yourself to complete forgiveness, God-directed change, and new hope for the future. Enjoy the freedom of a conscience clear from guilt. Sleep peacefully, and live joyfully.

Create in me a clean heart, O God,
and renew a right spirit within me.

PSALM 51:10 ESV

Good Plan

Most of us feel more secure with plan A when we have a plan B. Although we realize that plan B is second best, it's our acceptable option if plan A doesn't work out or we're met with an unexpected turn of events.

In matters of faith, however, God provides no plan B. If He is everything to us, then why do we look around for second sources of spiritual sustenance? Why do we gather things that we think will bring fulfillment, such as wealth, status, or popularity, just in case God doesn't come through for us? Why do we give a nod to other gods? We don't need anything more than what our God has laid out for us. Our heavenly Father has graciously given us the privilege of loving Him exclusively and finding in His plan everything sufficient for our spiritual security now and forever.

Imagine pledging your exclusive love to someone but all the while keeping another love in mind just in case your present love should desert you. The presence of a backup plan would make it impossible for you to give your whole self to the one you love. Your expression of love would be less than genuine and always tainted with the shadow of deception.

From you, God asks for willing, authentic, and exclusive love—the kind of love Jesus showed for you in His life, death, and resurrection. By believing in Him and Him alone, you will be able to enjoy the peace of mind and heart that only an honest relationship can bring. And there's one more thing: God's plan A comes with a guarantee: it will never fail.

No other gods, only me.

EXODUS 20:3 MSG

Helpless or Hopeless?

"He believed I could do it," Shannon says of her high school counselor. "He gave me something to hope for." Mr. Nelson had looked beyond her seeming nonchalance and apathy to find a frightened girl living with her frequently out-of-work mother and four younger siblings in a one-room apartment. Because Shannon felt ashamed of her situation, she avoided talking to her classmates or her teachers. Mr. Nelson's patience and caring, however, softened the wall of pretense she had built around her.

While Mr. Nelson could not change Shannon's difficult family life, he could do something even more beneficial—he could help her change her perception of herself and her situation. Once she realized that her worth as a person did not depend on outside circumstances, she began to believe in her talents and abilities. No more the victim, she started to find practical ways she could help the family stay together and become more stable. At her graduation ceremony, she walked proudly and confidently across the stage to accept her diploma. Her poise, maturity, and confidence far outstripped that of her classmates, and she was an inspiration to her brothers and sisters.

Your perception of yourself and the challenges you face makes the difference between remaining helpless or becoming hopeful. You have help because God is a God of love. He cares and understands your deepest needs. You have hope because God is a God of hope whose promises stand forever. How do you see yourself in His plan for you?

I will bless you with a future filled with hope—a future of success, not of suffering.

JEREMIAH 29:11 CEV

Challenged Faith

Regardless of our circumstances, faith is a challenge. When times are good and things are going the way we want, we're challenged to remember that God is the source of our comfort, accomplishments, and well-being. Finding ourselves blessed with everything we need, we easily forget our deepest spiritual needs. When times are bad and one misfortune after another comes our way, however, we're challenged to believe that God is still present and that He cares and understands. We feel frustrated and angry, wondering why we have to struggle so hard while others have it so easy. Yes, faith is a challenge, but not one we're ever expected to overcome on our own.

God's Spirit not only has planted faith in your heart but gives you the ability to believe in Him through all the ups and downs of life. His gifts of humility and gratitude allow you to delight in your many blessings, remembering they come not through your personal cleverness or wisdom, but through the hand of your gracious and generous God. His gifts of patience, trust, and perseverance enable you to come through difficulties, knowing that you can do so, not because of your strength, but His.

Faith's challenges show no preference for believers facing poverty or believers basking in luxury but come to all with equal force and severity. Right now, what thoughts or circumstances are testing your faith, hope, and trust in God? Pray for His Spirit to give you the strength you need to meet the specific challenges facing you today.

God is our refuge and strength,
an ever-present help in trouble.

PSALM 46:1 NIV

195

Wealth Management

Astute financial managers sometimes buy currently undervalued stock. Years of education, experience, and observation have given them insight, and they see signs that their investment now will yield dividends in the future.

Similarly, God-given spiritual insight gives us the ability to spot spiritual blessings hiding in unlikely places. He teaches us as we apply His guidelines to our lives and watch how He works with us and how He works in the lives of others. As we become spiritually experienced, we see our critical boss, irritating coworker, and domineering relative as opportunities to practice patience and good humor. Tough times, misfortune, and loss are chances to "invest" in perseverance and endurance. Discouragement and disappointment can draw us closer to God, who is our source of hope for the future. No temptation or difficult circumstance is undervalued for its potential to yield dividends of inner strength, firm character, and lasting resolve.

If you invest your money wisely, you don't expect instant

windfalls. Your kindness may not make a dent in someone else's rudeness, and your grace in rough situations may not get you out of them any faster than if you had reacted with bitterness and anger. But, unlike financial investments, your spiritual investments are guaranteed to grow and yield great returns in time. And occasionally, you might even get a bonus—like a genuine smile from that grump you meet at the vending machine every day!

There's potential spiritual wealth all around you. What's your investment strategy?

"He gives wisdom to the wise and knowledge to those who have understanding."

DANIEL 2:21 ESV

Grow Up

"It's God's will," the young teen would sigh. After years of consigning every setback to "God's will," she stopped trying to achieve. If God's will was going to happen anyway, why attempt anything? As she entered adulthood, she felt like a buoy carried by the capricious currents of the sea, enduring whatever others wanted her to do, or did to her, as "God's will."

Prolonged spiritual, as well as social, immaturity hinders healthy relationships. Socially, immaturity may express itself in shyness, insecurity, or lack of confidence. Spiritually, it often tries to cast a heavenly light on human weaknesses, like fear, feelings of powerlessness, or failure to put God-given abilities to use. Maturity comes with experience. We put ourselves in social situations and discover the rewards of healthy relationships with others. We learn more about God's way with people and grow to know the joy and comfort of a healthy relationship with God.

Mature acceptance of God's will allows you to see

challenges as vehicles to lift your relationship with Him to a higher level of trust and reliance. Yes, you make your plans, but you wholeheartedly embrace His, even though they might take you in a different direction. How is God's will working in your life right now? How do your thoughts and expectations reflect a mature relationship with Him?

So come on, let's leave the preschool fingerpainting exercises on Christ and get on with the grand work of art. Grow up in Christ.

HEBREWS 6:1 MSG

Great Escape

With every trouble, there is a way of escape, yet all but one draws even more trouble. Walking out on our legitimate, God-given responsibilities damages our reputation, weakens our character, and robs others of our participation and contributions. Deciding to use drugs or alcohol invites accidents, ill health, and broken relationships. Allowing despair to overcome us reveals lack of faith in God's care and control. The one positive method? Do it God's way. Whether He leads you over, around, or through your troubles, His way brings not further hardship, but increased blessings.

Escape with Him! Turn to your Lord in deep, fervent prayer, asking for eyes to see your situation clearly, ears to hear His voice, and feet willing to follow wherever He leads. Gain insight and understanding from people who can give you sound, wise advice. Examine your options. You can discern God's will in the choice that requires nothing contrary to His revealed truth in the Bible, inflicts no unnecessary hurt or hardship on yourself or someone else, and does not hinder healthy spiritual growth. Following Him may require your continued endurance or mean a difficult decision. Others may applaud your courage or shake their heads in bewilderment. The main thing is that you follow Him.

If you have ever handled trouble the wrong way, take from your experience a valuable lesson. If you have ever dealt with it the right way, highlight the blessings and benefits you now possess. Either way, let what you know from the past strengthen you as you meet life's challenges God's way—all the way.

I say, "Oh, that I had wings like a dove! I would fly away and be at rest."

PSALM 55:6 ESV

Sweet Music

No matter how well you might be able to play a violin, you can't correctly interpret Vivaldi's concertos for strings if you fail to tune your instrument. Your expertise on the keyboard hardly matters in performing Mozart's piano concertos if your piano hasn't been tuned. Similarly, your emotions aren't able to accurately reflect God's work in your life unless they're tuned to His will.

Left in their natural state, our emotions are unreliable. When we're feeling blue, or lonely, or discouraged, we'll instinctively decide that God disapproves of us, despite the fact we may be faithfully following Him and gathering blessing after blessing with every step. When we're feeling happy, we figure God is quite pleased with us, yet it's possible that He's patiently waiting for us to realize that we're ignoring His loud and clear call. In both cases, our emotions were out of tune with the truth.

Spirit-tuned emotions turn you toward Him, not away from Him. Say you feel little appreciated after having done a kindness—His Spirit quiets bitterness with the knowledge that you have applied the faith of your heart to the work of your hands. When others batter at your emotions with unmerited criticism, He quells natural anger with the joy of having listened to Him instead of the world.

Are your emotions in tune? Let His Spirit bring sweet music to your soul.

You will keep in perfect peace all who trust in you, all whose thoughts are fixed on you!

ISAIAH 26:3 NLT

Living Faith

Living faith is all-consuming faith. Though the Holy Spirit plants and nurtures your faith unseen in the depths of your heart, it doesn't hide. It's not content to remain as a fine ideal, and it won't let you display it only around those who approve. Living faith refuses to stay as a private exercise, settle in the background, or wait for the future to show itself in your life. When faith is kindled, it's like a fire you can't contain!

The flames of faith leave their mark in your thoughts and on your words and actions. In red-hot faith's presence, idle, hurtful, or negative thoughts are burned to cinders. You don't want them because they no longer bring satisfaction or reflect your beliefs. Gossip, unkind words, and needless criticisms lose their power to control you, and willful wrongdoing holds no appeal.

Only you and God know how genuine, how strong, your faith really is. But everyone around you knows if you meet your challenges with patience and hope; celebrate your successes with thanksgiving and humility; keep your decisions in line with God's commandments; act kindly, generously, and thoughtfully around others; exhibit tolerance and good humor; and help, comfort, and encourage others in practical and meaningful ways. When your faith is alive, it shines as brightly on the outside as it does on the inside.

Inside your heart, the flame of faith is burning. Think of how it lights your path, shines in your actions, and warms your relationships. In what specific ways could you fan its flame?

For this reason I remind you to fan into flame the gift of God.

2 TIMOTHY 1:6 NIV

Why Not?

You never know until you try. Reading about the lives of notable Christians—and there are many—isn't the same as following the same guiding light in your own life. Watching believers around you will show you many examples—some excellent and some that could be better, for sure. But observation isn't the same as experience, and experience comes only by trying the Christian walk yourself.

If you regularly take time to meditate on a meaningful phrase or contemplate the beauty of creation, you already know the peace of body and mind these practices bring. Why not now center your thoughts on the truths of scripture and hear the voice of your God calling your name, calling you back, calling you closer to Him? He offers peace for your soul! If you want higher spiritual understanding, increased spiritual wisdom, and solid spiritual sustenance, you're already ready to reach, learn, and grow. Why not reach for your heavenly Father, who stretches His arms out to you? Why not learn about Jesus Christ, whose life, death, and resurrection impacts your life now and forever? Why not invite the Holy Spirit into your heart? Enabled by the nourishment He will give you, your relationship with God will grow—that's His promise!

By God's good will, you are at this point on your spiritual path. Now He calls you to take the next step, committing your all to Him. Waiting until a future time simply puts off to another day the blessings He has in store for you today. Asking "Why me?" may make Him smile as He asks you in return, *"Why not you?"*

Come, accept His invitation to a lasting, life-changing relationship with Him. You'll never know its joys, challenges, triumphs, comfort, freedom, empowerment, and peace until you go ahead and try it for yourself.

Those who trust the LORD will find new strength. They will be strong like eagles soaring upward on wings.

Isaiah 40:31 cev

Scripture Index

New Testament

Matthew

Read Through the Bible in a Year

1-Jan	Gen. 1-2	Matt. 1	Ps. 1
2-Jan	Gen. 3-4	Matt. 2	Ps. 2
3-Jan	Gen. 5-7	Matt. 3	Ps. 3
4-Jan	Gen. 8-10	Matt. 4	Ps. 4
5-Jan	Gen. 11-13	Matt. 5:1-20	Ps. 5
6-Jan	Gen. 14-16	Matt. 5:21-48	Ps. 6
7-Jan	Gen. 17-18	Matt. 6:1-18	Ps. 7
8-Jan	Gen. 19-20	Matt. 6:19-34	Ps. 8
9-Jan	Gen. 21-23	Matt. 7:1-11	Ps. 9:1-8
10-Jan	Gen. 24	Matt. 7:12-29	Ps. 9:9-20
11-Jan	Gen. 25-26	Matt. 8:1-17	Ps. 10:1-11
12-Jan	Gen. 27:1-28:9	Matt. 8:18-34	Ps. 10:12-18
13-Jan	Gen. 28:10-29:35	Matt. 9	Ps. 11
14-Jan	Gen. 30:1-31:21	Matt. 10:1-15	Ps. 12
15-Jan	Gen. 31:22-32:21	Matt. 10:16-36	Ps. 13
16-Jan	Gen. 32:22-34:31	Matt. 10:37-11:6	Ps. 14
17-Jan	Gen. 35-36	Matt. 11:7-24	Ps. 15
18-Jan	Gen. 37-38	Matt. 11:25-30	Ps. 16
19-Jan	Gen. 39-40	Matt. 12:1-29	Ps. 17
20-Jan	Gen. 41	Matt. 12:30-50	Ps. 18:1-15
21-Jan	Gen. 42-43	Matt. 13:1-9	Ps. 18:16-29
22-Jan	Gen. 44-45	Matt. 13:10-23	Ps. 18:30-50
23-Jan	Gen. 46:1-47:26	Matt. 13:24-43	Ps. 19
24-Jan	Gen. 47:27-49:28	Matt. 13:44-58	Ps. 20
25-Jan	Gen. 49:29-Exod. 1:22	Matt. 14	Ps. 21
26-Jan	Exod. 2-3	Matt. 15:1-28	Ps. 22:1-21
27-Jan	Exod. 4:1-5:21	Matt. 15:29-16:12	Ps. 22:22-31
28-Jan	Exod. 5:22-7:24	Matt. 16:13-28	Ps. 23
29-Jan	Exod. 7:25-9:35	Matt. 17:1-9	Ps. 24
30-Jan	Exod. 10-11	Matt. 17:10-27	Ps. 25
31-Jan	Exod. 12	Matt. 18:1-20	Ps. 26
1-Feb	Exod. 13-14	Matt. 18:21-35	Ps. 27
2-Feb	Exod. 15-16	Matt. 19:1-15	Ps. 28
3-Feb	Exod. 17-19	Matt. 19:16-30	Ps. 29

4-Feb	Exod. 20-21	Matt. 20:1-19	Ps. 30
5-Feb	Exod. 22-23	Matt. 20:20-34	Ps. 31:1-8
6-Feb	Exod. 24-25	Matt. 21:1-27	Ps. 31:9-18
7-Feb	Exod 26-27	Matt. 21:28-46	Ps. 31:19-24
8-Feb	Exod. 28	Matt. 22	Ps. 32
9-Feb	Exod. 29	Matt. 23:1-36	Ps. 33:1-12
10-Feb	Exod. 30-31	Matt. 23:37-24:28	Ps. 33:13-22
11-Feb	Exod. 32-33	Matt. 24:29-51	Ps. 34:1-7
12-Feb	Exod. 34:1-35:29	Matt. 25:1-13	Ps. 34:8-22
13-Feb	Exod. 35:30-37:29	Matt. 25:14-30	Ps. 35:1-8
14-Feb	Exod. 38-39	Matt. 25:31-46	Ps. 35:9-17
15-Feb	Exod. 40	Matt. 26:1-35	Ps. 35:18-28
16-Feb	Lev. 1-3	Matt. 26:36-68	Ps. 36:1-6
17-Feb	Lev. 4:1-5:13	Matt. 26:69-27:26	Ps. 36:7-12
18-Feb	Lev. 5:14 -7:21	Matt. 27:27-50	Ps. 37:1-6
19-Feb	Lev. 7:22-8:36	Matt. 27:51-66	Ps. 37:7-26
20-Feb	Lev. 9-10	Matt. 28	Ps. 37:27-40
21-Feb	Lev. 11-12	Mark 1:1-28	Ps. 38
22-Feb	Lev. 13	Mark 1:29-39	Ps. 39
23-Feb	Lev. 14	Mark 1:40-2:12	Ps. 40:1-8
24-Feb	Lev. 15	Mark 2:13-3:35	Ps. 40:9-17
25-Feb	Lev. 16-17	Mark 4:1-20	Ps. 41:1-4
26-Feb	Lev. 18-19	Mark 4:21-41	Ps. 41:5-13
27-Feb	Lev. 20	Mark 5	Ps. 42-43
28-Feb	Lev. 21-22	Mark 6:1-13	Ps. 44
1-Mar	Lev. 23-24	Mark 6:14-29	Ps. 45:1-5
2-Mar	Lev. 25	Mark 6:30-56	Ps. 45:6-12
3-Mar	Lev. 26	Mark 7	Ps. 45:13-17
4-Mar	Lev. 27	Mark 8	Ps. 46
5-Mar	Num. 1-2	Mark 9:1-13	Ps. 47
6-Mar	Num. 3	Mark 9:14-50	Ps. 48:1-8
7-Mar	Num. 4	Mark 10:1-34	Ps. 48:9-14
8-Mar	Num. 5:1-6:21	Mark 10:35-52	Ps. 49:1-9
9-Mar	Num. 6:22-7:47	Mark 11	Ps. 49:10-20
10-Mar	Num. 7:48-8:4	Mark 12:1-27	Ps. 50:1-15
11-Mar	Num. 8:5-9:23	Mark 12:28-44	Ps. 50:16-23

12-Mar	Num. 10-11	Mark 13:1-8	Ps. 51:1-9
13-Mar	Num. 12-13	Mark 13:9-37	Ps. 51:10-19
14-Mar	Num. 14	Mark 14:1-31	Ps. 52
15-Mar	Num. 15	Mark 14:32-72	Ps. 53
16-Mar	Num. 16	Mark 15:1-32	Ps. 54
17-Mar	Num. 17-18	Mark 15:33-47	Ps. 55
18-Mar	Num. 19-20	Mark 16	Ps. 56:1-7
19-Mar	Num. 21:1-22:20	Luke 1:1-25	Ps. 56:8-13
20-Mar	Num. 22:21-23:30	Luke 1:26-56	Ps. 57
21-Mar	Num. 24-25	Luke 1:57-2:20	Ps. 58
22-Mar	Num. 26:1-27:11	Luke 2:21-38	Ps. 59:1-8
23-Mar	Num. 27:12-29:11	Luke 2:39-52	Ps. 59:9-17
24-Mar	Num. 29:12-30:16	Luke 3	Ps. 60:1-5
25-Mar	Num. 31	Luke 4	Ps. 60:6-12
26-Mar	Num. 32-33	Luke 5:1-16	Ps. 61
27-Mar	Num. 34-36	Luke 5:17-32	Ps. 62:1-6
28-Mar	Deut. 1:1-2:25	Luke 5:33-6:11	Ps. 62:7-12
29-Mar	Deut. 2:26-4:14	Luke 6:12-35	Ps. 63:1-5
30-Mar	Deut. 4:15-5:22	Luke 6:36-49	Ps. 63:6-11
31-Mar	Deut. 5:23-7:26	Luke 7:1-17	Ps. 64:1-5
1-Apr	Deut. 8-9	Luke 7:18-35	Ps. 64:6-10
2-Apr	Deut. 10-11	Luke 7:36-8:3	Ps. 65:1-8
3-Apr	Deut. 12-13	Luke 8:4-21	Ps. 65:9-13
4-Apr	Deut. 14:1-16:8	Luke 8:22-39	Ps. 66:1-7
5-Apr	Deut. 16:9-18:22	Luke 8:40-56	Ps. 66:8-15
6-Apr	Deut. 19:1-21:9	Luke 9:1-22	Ps. 66:16-20
7-Apr	Deut. 21:10-23:8	Luke 9:23-42	Ps. 67
8-Apr	Deut. 23:9-25:19	Luke 9:43-62	Ps. 68:1-6
9-Apr	Deut. 26:1-28:14	Luke 10:1-20	Ps. 68:7-14
10-Apr	Deut. 28:15-68	Luke 10:21-37	Ps. 68:15-19
11-Apr	Deut. 29-30	Luke 10:38-11:23	Ps. 68:20-27
12-Apr	Deut. 31:1-32:22	Luke 11:24-36	Ps. 68:28-35
13-Apr	Deut. 32:23-33:29	Luke 11:37-54	Ps. 69:1-9
14-Apr	Deut. 34-Josh. 2	Luke 12:1-15	Ps. 69:10-17
15-Apr	Josh. 3:1-5:12	Luke 12:16-40	Ps. 69:18-28
16-Apr	Josh. 5:13-7:26	Luke 12:41-48	Ps. 69:29-36

17-Apr	Josh. 8-9	Luke 12:49-59	Ps. 70
18-Apr	Josh. 10:1-11:15	Luke 13:1-21	Ps. 71:1-6
19-Apr	Josh. 11:16-13:33	Luke 13:22-35	Ps. 71:7-16
20-Apr	Josh. 14-16	Luke 14:1-15	Ps. 71:17-21
21-Apr	Josh. 17:1-19:16	Luke 14:16-35	Ps. 71:22-24
22-Apr	Josh. 19:17-21:42	Luke 15:1-10	Ps. 72:1-11
23-Apr	Josh. 21:43-22:34	Luke 15:11-32	Ps. 72:12-20
24-Apr	Josh. 23-24	Luke 16:1-18	Ps. 73:1-9
25-Apr	Judg. 1-2	Luke 16:19-17:10	Ps. 73:10-20
26-Apr	Judg. 3-4	Luke 17:11-37	Ps. 73:21-28
27-Apr	Judg. 5:1-6:24	Luke 18:1-17	Ps. 74:1-3
28-Apr	Judg. 6:25-7:25	Luke 18:18-43	Ps. 74:4-11
29-Apr	Judg. 8:1-9:23	Luke 19:1-28	Ps. 74:12-17
30-Apr	Judg. 9:24-10:18	Luke 19:29-48	Ps. 74:18-23
1-May	Judg. 11:1-12:7	Luke 20:1-26	Ps. 75:1-7
2-May	Judg. 12:8-14:20	Luke 20:27-47	Ps. 75:8-10
3-May	Judg. 15-16	Luke 21:1-19	Ps. 76:1-7
4-May	Judg. 17-18	Luke 21:20-22:6	Ps. 76:8-12
5-May	Judg. 19:1-20:23	Luke 22:7-30	Ps. 77:1-11
6-May	Judg. 20:24-21:25	Luke 22:31-54	Ps. 77:12-20
7-May	Ruth 1-2	Luke 22:55-23:25	Ps. 78:1-4
8-May	Ruth 3-4	Luke 23:26-24:12	Ps. 78:5-8
9-May	1 Sam. 1:1-2:21	Luke 24:13-53	Ps. 78:9-16
10-May	1 Sam. 2:22-4:22	John 1:1-28	Ps. 78:17-24
11-May	1 Sam. 5-7	John 1:29-51	Ps. 78:25-33
12-May	1 Sam. 8:1-9:26	John 2	Ps. 78:34-41
13-May	1 Sam. 9:27-11:15	John 3:1-22	Ps. 78:42-55
14-May	1 Sam. 12-13	John 3:23-4:10	Ps. 78:56-66
15-May	1 Sam. 14	John 4:11-38	Ps. 78:67-72
16-May	1 Sam. 15-16	John 4:39-54	Ps. 79:1-7
17-May	1 Sam. 17	John 5:1-24	Ps. 79:8-13
18-May	1 Sam. 18-19	John 5:25-47	Ps. 80:1-7
19-May	1 Sam. 20-21	John 6:1-21	Ps. 80:8-19
20-May	1 Sam. 22-23	John 6:22-42	Ps. 81:1-10
21-May	1 Sam. 24:1-25:31	John 6:43-71	Ps. 81:11-16
22-May	1 Sam. 25:32-27:12	John 7:1-24	Ps. 82

23-May	1 Sam. 28-29	John 7:25-8:11	Ps. 83
24-May	1 Sam. 30-31	John 8:12-47	Ps. 84:1-4
25-May	2 Sam. 1-2	John 8:48-9:12	Ps. 84:5-12
26-May	2 Sam. 3-4	John 9:13-34	Ps. 85:1-7
27-May	2 Sam. 5:1-7:17	John 9:35-10:10	Ps. 85:8-13
28-May	2 Sam. 7:18-10:19	John 10:11-30	Ps. 86:1-10
29-May	2 Sam. 11:1-12:25	John 10:31-11:16	Ps. 86:11-17
30-May	2 Sam. 12:26-13:39	John 11:17-54	Ps. 87
31-May	2 Sam. 14:1-15:12	John 11:55-12:19	Ps. 88:1-9
1-Jun	2 Sam. 15:13-16:23	John 12:20-43	Ps. 88:10-18
2-Jun	2 Sam. 17:1-18:18	John 12:44-13:20	Ps. 89:1-6
3-Jun	2 Sam. 18:19-19:39	John 13:21-38	Ps. 89:7-13
4-Jun	2 Sam. 19:40-21:22	John 14:1-17	Ps. 89:14-18
5-Jun	2 Sam. 22:1-23:7	John 14:18-15:27	Ps. 89:19-29
6-Jun	2 Sam. 23:8-24:25	John 16:1-22	Ps. 89:30-37
7-Jun	1 Kings 1	John 16:23-17:5	Ps. 89:38-52
8-Jun	1 Kings 2	John 17:6-26	Ps. 90:1-12
9-Jun	1 Kings 3-4	John 18:1-27	Ps. 90:13-17
10-Jun	1 Kings 5-6	John 18:28-19:5	Ps. 91:1-10
11-Jun	1 Kings 7	John 19:6-25a	Ps. 91:11-16
12-Jun	1 Kings 8:1-53	John 19:25b-42	Ps. 92:1-9
13-Jun	1 Kings 8:54-10:13	John 20:1-18	Ps. 92:10-15
14-Jun	1 Kings 10:14-11:43	John 20:19-31	Ps. 93
15-Jun	1 Kings 12:1-13:10	John 21	Ps. 94:1-11
16-Jun	1 Kings 13:11-14:31	Acts 1:1-11	Ps. 94:12-23
17-Jun	1 Kings 15:1-16:20	Acts 1:12-26	Ps. 95
18-Jun	1 Kings 16:21-18:19	Acts 2:1-21	Ps. 96:1-8
19-Jun	1 Kings 18:20-19:21	Acts2:22-41	Ps. 96:9-13
20-Jun	1 Kings 20	Acts 2:42-3:26	Ps. 97:1-6
21-Jun	1 Kings 21:1-22:28	Acts 4:1-22	Ps. 97:7-12
22-Jun	1 Kings 22:29- 2 Kings 1:18	Acts 4:23-5:11	Ps. 98
23-Jun	2 Kings 2-3	Acts 5:12-28	Ps. 99
24-Jun	2 Kings 4	Acts 5:29-6:15	Ps. 100
25-Jun	2 Kings 5:1-6:23	Acts 7:1-16	Ps. 101
26-Jun	2 Kings 6:24-8:15	Acts 7:17-36	Ps. 102:1-7

27-Jun	2 Kings 8:16-9:37	Acts 7:37-53	Ps. 102:8-17
28-Jun	2 Kings 10-11	Acts 7:54-8:8	Ps. 102:18-28
29-Jun	2 Kings 12-13	Acts 8:9-40	Ps. 103:1-9
30-Jun	2 Kings 14-15	Acts 9:1-16	Ps. 103:10-14
1-Jul	2 Kings 16-17	Acts 9:17-31	Ps. 103:15-22
2-Jul	2 Kings 18:1-19:7	Acts 9:32-10:16	Ps. 104:1-9
3-Jul	2 Kings 19:8-20:21	Acts 10:17-33	Ps. 104:10-23
4-Jul	2 Kings 21:1-22:20	Acts 10:34-11:18	Ps. 104: 24-30
5-Jul	2 Kings 23	Acts 11:19-12:17	Ps. 104:31-35
6-Jul	2 Kings 24-25	Acts 12:18-13:13	Ps. 105:1-7
7-Jul	1 Chron. 1-2	Acts 13:14-43	Ps. 105:8-15
8-Jul	1 Chron. 3:1-5:10	Acts 13:44-14:10	Ps. 105:16-28
9-Jul	1 Chron. 5:11-6:81	Acts 14:11-28	Ps. 105:29-36
10-Jul	1 Chron. 7:1-9:9	Acts 15:1-18	Ps. 105:37-45
11-Jul	1 Chron. 9:10-11:9	Acts 15:19-41	Ps. 106:1-12
12-Jul	1 Chron. 11:10-12:40	Acts 16:1-15	Ps. 106:13-27
13-Jul	1 Chron. 13-15	Acts 16:16-40	Ps. 106:28-33
14-Jul	1 Chron. 16-17	Acts 17:1-14	Ps. 106:34-43
15-Jul	1 Chron. 18-20	Acts 17:15-34	Ps. 106:44-48
16-Jul	1 Chron. 21-22	Acts 18:1-23	Ps. 107:1-9
17-Jul	1 Chron. 23-25	Acts 18:24-19:10	Ps. 107:10-16
18-Jul	1 Chron. 26-27	Acts 19:11-22	Ps. 107:17-32
19-Jul	1 Chron. 28-29	Acts 19:23-41	Ps. 107:33-38
20-Jul	2 Chron. 1-3	Acts 20:1-16	Ps. 107:39-43
21-Jul	2 Chron. 4:1-6:11	Acts 20:17-38	Ps. 108
22-Jul	2 Chron. 6:12-7:10	Acts 21:1-14	Ps. 109:1-20
23-Jul	2 Chron. 7:11-9:28	Acts 21:15-32	Ps. 109:21-31
24-Jul	2 Chron. 9:29-12:16	Acts 21:33-22:16	Ps. 110:1-3
25-Jul	2 Chron. 13-15	Acts 22:17-23:11	Ps. 110:4-7
26-Jul	2 Chron. 16-17	Acts 23:12-24:21	Ps. 111
27-Jul	2 Chron. 18-19	Acts 24:22-25:12	Ps. 112
28-Jul	2 Chron. 20-21	Acts 25:13-27	Ps. 113
29-Jul	2 Chron. 22-23	Acts 26	Ps. 114
30-Jul	2 Chron. 24:1-25:16	Acts 27:1-20	Ps. 115:1-10
31-Jul	2 Chron. 25:17-27:9	Acts 27:21-28:6	Ps. 115:11-18
1-Aug	2 Chron. 28:1-29:19	Acts 28:7-31	Ps. 116:1-5